THE CLUB OF TRUE CREATORS

(*Klub istinskih stvaralaca*)

MILAN TRIPKOVIĆ

English Translation, Rossum Press, 2023

This is a work of fiction. All of the characters, organizations, and events portrayed are either products of the author's imagination or are used fictitiously.

Rossum Press ISBN 979-8-9896152-0-9

Originally published in Serbia as *Klub istinskih svaralaca* by Fabrika knjiga.

First published in the United States by Rossum Press.

First Rossum Press Edition: December 2023

1

THE TALE OF THE Club of True Creators begins in front of a mirror. No, not one of those magic mirrors that gaslights you about how pretty you are, but rather a large, ordinary looking glass hanging on a bedroom closet door which is currently reflecting a man in his late fifties. He has been playing a guitar for the past half-hour.

While there's nothing particularly notable about this, we do immediately observe that the man is wearing nothing but a pair of red clogs. More notable perhaps, is that a busty, scantily-clad woman is filming him with her phone from a low, surreptitious angle. Most notably of all, is that the man and woman seem to share a deeply serious approach to this whole encounter. In fact, we'd dare to say that the man looks irritated—he isn't, apparently, being framed properly by his camerawoman.

"Don't film from there, how many times do I have to tell you?! It'll *show!*" he whines.

"It won't. And you look taller this way."

"Taller, yeah, but..."

He waves his hand vaguely and plays with the guitar's strap to adjust its height. He starts up again, and we realise that it was a grave mistake to call the man's activity "playing." The notes we hear are so dull and dissonant that anyone in possession of an undisturbed musical sense would cover their ears. And, as if that were not enough, he now begins to sing. No amount of ear-covering can save us now; his caterwauling voice, struggling in vain for a melody, pierces straight to our ear canals. There, it continues to resonate, inducing virtually clinical nausea and an acute sense of vertigo. We await the final notes in desperation, holding each other fast so that our knees won't give out. The believers among us urgently pray that God either silence the man, or strike them deaf.

"*Where there's fire, there's smoke, I can feel it, the tide's coming innnnn...*"

He accentuates the end, stretching the last note to the point of absurdity.

"*.......nnnnnnnnnn!*"

The négligéed camerawoman lowers her phone and applauds enthusiastically. This leads us to wonder, and take a closer look: Does this woman in fact have ears? (She does. The search for explanation continues.)

"It was all right, eh?" he asks, a gesture at humility.

"Perfect!" she assents.

"Really?"

"Absolutely! You'll see."

"Great. Send me the video."

"Will do!"

"I'm going to get dressed; I'm freezing. My suit's hanging on the bathtub, right?"

"Hold on, aren't we going to..."

"What?"

"I mean..."

"Sorry babe, I really can't now. Gotta go. I have an important meeting in fifteen minutes. How about tomorrow?"

"But you said..."

"Tomorrow."

And so he leaves his camerawoman behind. Although she's transparently disappointed by his premature departure, it seems unlikely to be the first time. Rising from the floor, she removes a pair of earplugs and sits on the edge of the bed. Perhaps there are some among us who would rather stay and console this scantily-clad woman but, since our protagonist has left the scene, we are duty-bound to follow. Probably, we're about to learn something about the Club of True Creators in this meeting he mentioned.

He strolls down the street at a leisurely pace. A bowler hat rests squarely on his head, his eyes hidden behind glasses with thick, John Lennon-style lenses. His olive-green coat nearly touches the ground, rendering only a strip of his wide blue velvet pants visible above steel-toed, black cowboy boots. Between hairs of his greying beard nestle some pastry crumbs. He pauses by a chestnut tree in the park, touches its bark, and thoughtfully observes the canopy overhead. He bends to pick up a fallen chestnut, examines it from all angles, sniffs it a couple times, and pockets it. It would seem that our protagonist's "meeting" was a nothing but a half-hearted fib to evade his previously agreed commitment. He sits down gingerly on a nearby bench. Crossing his left leg over his right, he rests a hand on his face and allows his gaze to drift into the middle distance.

Now is the perfect time to delve into the inner world of our hero.

Gassy, gassy, gassy! This pastry makes me so bloated. What the hell do they put in it? He pulls out a notebook and begins to write. A couple minutes later, feeling a chill, he thrusts his hands in his pockets, rises, and paces on, crossing the grass. Lost in thought, he remains ignorant of two girls walking a cocker spaniel a few paces behind him. And, in that ignorance, he lets out a loud fart. He notices them giggling, but tries his best to hide his embarrassment. He lowers his eyes, and continues forward with dignity. Leaving the park, he stops by a newsstand: cigarettes, Sudoku, and today's *Večernje Novosti*.[1] Then, he ambles down the boulevard to the train station. He observes the platforms through the grimy glass walls of the waiting area. His expression is focussed, and he shifts his weight from left to right when his back starts to ache from standing. Patiently, our protagonist waits for inspiration to strike. It always does here. And then, indeed, there it is! The thoughtful scowl begins to soften into a smile, as he takes out his notebook...

---

1. "The Evening News," the leading Serbian tabloid newspaper.

"DO YOU WANT A BLOWJOB FOR TWO HUNDRED DINARS?" A woman with blunt features and sunken eyes materialises, an on-duty independent entrepreneur of the station. She's not especially attractive, but she is direct.

"I'm sorry?"

"Suck your cock? We can go to the loo if you want, or the park if you prefer to have an audience."

"Ah, I see. No, thank you."

"All right then, one-fifty."

"It's not about the price, I'm afraid, it's just..."

"One-twenty?"

"I'm not..."

"I'll show you my pussy."

"But..."

"You can touch my tits."

"Stay away from me."

"Fifty?"

"No! Are you deaf or just ugly?! Even if you paid *me* fifty *thousand*, I would never! Got it? Not if I was stuck with no other company for months on end!" He turns his back angrily and faces the platform, so doesn't see her chin begin to quiver, or her eyes fill with tears. She just stands behind him, silent and still. A whole minute she stands there, perhaps even two, before walking away. At the ticket booth, there's no one to pity her, no one to scowl at him in condemnation. We take the opportunity to do so ourselves, before the story pushes this sad encounter heartlessly into vague memory. Oblivious to our scowls, the man returns his gaze to his notebook for a long while, pencil in hand, frown on lips, and hesitates to write down the line that had so delighted him earlier—it no longer passes the "first line of a poem" test. He murmurs the line under his breath, hums the syllables to himself, and grips the pencil as if to squeeze the *mots justes* out of it, but still—nothing. It's hopeless. He gives up for the time being and goes to the station pub to grab a coffee and read his newspaper, but is overwhelmed by an immediately if nebulously hostile atmosphere at the bar. So great is the discomfort that he immediately turns to leave.

"Vojo!"

He visibly flinches at hearing his name. Our protagonist hovers at the door and, for the next several seconds, tries to determine to whom the voice belongs. Nothing yet, but...

"Vojo, man!"

He contemplates whether to simply beat a hasty retreat—he's near the exit, and could perhaps make a run for it. However, fatefully, his curiosity gets the better of him, and he turns around at the last moment. He can just make out a figure waving from a corner but not much else due to the smoke which fills the room. As he walks toward the table in the corner of the bar, our protagonist is acutely aware that he's the centre of the entire pub's attention. Except perhaps for one drunk who's sprawled over a table; we think he's asleep. He thinks of that moment in a Western when a stranger enters the saloon, instantly extinguishing the chatter of the local gunslingers. Only in this joint, the stranger is the only one wearing cowboy boots.

"What's the matter, Vojo, you don't remember me?" The figure, which has since resolved into a large man, stands up and warmly extends a hand.

"Er, Nikola?" he hazards, squinting at the still entirely unfamiliar face.

"Nikola who? It's Pešut, man! Rajko Pešut, we served together in Ljubljana."

"Oh, it's you, Rajko..." He says, allowing himself to be pulled into Pešut's hearty bear hug. It feels great, honestly. The embrace sends shivers down his spine, he could purr like a cat. He tries to recall the last person to hug him so warmly and is certain it was his mother, who passed away twenty years ago. Unfortunately, there has been a mix-up. Our protagonist has never been to Ljubljana, nor has he served in the military. He'd been exempted from military service due to good fortune and poor eyesight. After briefly ruminating over the incredible coincidence that he should share the name Vojislav with Pešut's army buddy, he considers how best to extract himself from this mess.

"Who would've thought? I met crazy Muamer outside the German embassy in Belgrade two weeks ago, and we laughed about the time you shoved a gun into Žurić's mouth in the guardhouse. 'Shut it already, you Montenegrin chatterbox!'" Pešut laughs robustly as he recalls the incident and at last releases our protagonist from his embrace.

Vojislav tries to laugh along but can't quite manage. "Well..."

"That Žurić never did stop talking..."

"Rajko..."

"Come on, sit down. Why are you standing? Let's have a drink, catch up!"

"I have a meeting in fifteen minutes," he says, reheating his earlier excuse and composing a face of deepest regret. "I really should get going."

"Oh, come on, you can spare five minutes for your old comrade!"

Perhaps it's Pešut's commanding baritone or his even more commanding physique but, after a momentary wobble of indecision, Vojislav takes a seat. Pešut signals the waiter, orders drinks: a brandy, a caffè americano (no milk), and two seltzers. The drinks arrive promptly, and they toast. Pešut insists on the toast, although Vojislav himself is a teetotaler—the soldier's philosophy being that one toasts with a person, not the contents of one's glass.

Pešut's tales of shared military adventures and R&R in Ljubljana quickly become unbearable for our hero. A nagging pain pierces his temples as he smiles vacantly and nods in agreement with whatever is being said. Vojislav glances at his watch, fidgets in his seat, nervously alternates between coffee and seltzer. A vague itch strikes him just before noticing a face at the bar observing him sternly. The stranger's face remains myopically blurry to our protagonist...but he's positive that it's unknown to him. A fan maybe? someone who recognizes his face from a dust jacket or album cover, waiting for the right moment to approach and strike up a conversation. Eschewing false modesty, Vojislav concludes that he is, after all, one of Novi Sad's most distinguished writers. It wouldn't be a great surprise. As Pešut continues to ramble, our protagonist considers the possible intentions of the man at the bar, a knot forming in his stomach. He assesses the scene, reviews body language, and plumbs the inky darkness of the stranger's eyes. Maybe it's all in his head, who knows? As is so often the case, Vojislav's attempt at discretion has the opposite effect. As our protagonist twists his full head to a right angle, a schoolkid copying a neighbour's answer, would anyone actually be fooled?

His heart pounds when his eyes meet the stranger's. There's no longer any doubt that he's being watched, but the question remains: *why* is he being watched, and who is this guy at the bar working for? Vojislav ponders. It was only a matter of time until his literary ventures became a thorn in someone's side.

In the murky world of self-absorbed literati and towering authorial ego, Vojislav carries a heavy responsibility—to be the beacon, the creator of new realms, burdened with a genius comparable only to Pavić in the Serbian canon.[2] He has long feared that his mediocre colleagues' envy would curdle into something more sinister, False Creators bereft of imagination. The only question is what form their attack might take. How far they'd go. Although a man of peace, our protagonist feels he can defend himself if need be. After mentally weighing his yellow

---

2. Milorad Pavić, best known for his experimental but popular novel, Dictionary of the Khazars.

belt in judo, however, he interrupts Pešut midway through his story about a certain Sgt Prostran. Since they have so much left to cover, Vojislav suggests that they take a walk; the ex-soldier enthusiastically agrees and continues his story as he pulls on his jacket. Awkwardness aside, Pešut's company would be a powerful deterrent to any would-be attacker.

"Hey, Vojo, don't mess around. My invitation, my treat," Pešut says, mildly irritated that his story was interrupted at the exact moment when Prostran, absolutely plastered, rolls into the guardhouse at two in the morning. He'd planned to sleep in the barracks, since his wife wouldn't let him in. But the checkpoint was empty, as the duty soldier had skipped town to fool around with a female soldier in Pinca.

Had Pešut not insisted so forcefully on paying, Vojislav's own protests would almost certainly have been more muted. The man at the bar continues to stare, and our hero is on full alert. Fists clenched and already planning his first blow. As they pass the bar, however, the stranger comes into focus—as do his milky eyes, and the thin white can on which he is leaning. What a relief! Gratitude and joy wash over him like the Danube coursing through its channels. They exit the pub.

Outside, dusk has settled. Pešut continues his monologue—we're surprised that this guy ever retired to begin with, seeing as he had such a good time in the army. Suddenly, a commotion from within our ranks. The impatient among us demand that we first learn everything we can about the Club of True Creators. We're almost a full chapter in and, since Vojislav's meeting was a fabrication, none the wiser.

This demand for answers, mostly from the youth, becomes too loud to ignore, so we must momentarily leave our two pedestrians at № 6 Liberation Boulevard, just in front of the Intesa bank, and type into Google: c-l-u-b-o-f-t-r-u-e-c-r-e-a-t-o-r-s. The results are not encouraging. We see that there's a domain *stvaraoci.rs* but, when we click it, there's nothing but a logo with the notice: "Under construction."

"The Club of True Creators"

The second result is a Facebook group of the same name. There, below a brief description, several photos have been posted which feature Vojislav "Voja" Počuča with a hodgepodge of artists, critics, and academics. The description reads: "The Club of True Creators is an association of Novi Sad artists, formed in response to the scourge of political correctness, systemic mediocrity, and the moral turpitude which threatens the motherland." One sentence. We observe that the group has no members aside from Voja Počuča, the group administrator, despite being established over three years ago. It would seem that Voja's criteria for membership are stringent indeed. The remaining search results mostly relate to the Krušedol Synod, specifically the "Krušedol Bells" held by the Krajina People's Church Assembly on May 25, 2018.

According to Google, the guest of honour was a leading politician from Republika Srpska, and one of the "truest creators" and guardians of the region.[3] Most of the photo results also relate to this event, and show the Right Reverend Bishop Vasilije of Srem, surrounded by various groups of people. There's also a photo there from the premiere of Emir Kusturica's film *On the Milky Road* at FEST 2017, taken from an article in *Nova srpska politička misao*.[4] This leads us to an article by Nikola Tanasić which opines: "*Although an unmistakably excellent film, with impeccable direction, cinematography, music, and performances, it diverges from the familiar frames of Kusturica's imagination. The audience reaction was muted.*"

Suddenly, a deafening screech of brakes, followed by a dull thud.

---

3. One of two autonomous regions in the state of Bosnia & Herzegovina. Republika Srpska is majority Serb, while the other region (the Federation of Bosnia and Herzegovina) is Bosniak-majority with a sizable Croat minority.

4. "New Serbian Political Thought," a quarterly magazine which covers policy and politics from a mostly pro-establishment perspective.

We are yanked back down to Liberation Boulevard in Novi Sad, where a pedestrian has just been struck at an intersection near the Jeftinoće Tunnel. Voja Počuča, with hands in his pockets, stands above Pešut, the upper half of whose body is visible underneath a grey Punto. In the driver's seat, a woman grips the steering wheel with wide-eyed shock. Some witnesses hasten to call an ambulance, while a couple passersby rush to the injured man's aid. Voja, meanwhile, with legs of lead, stares blankly at the driver. A brief eternity passes before he realises that he is actually acquainted with the person behind the windshield. He springs to life and flees amidst the gathering post-accident chaos. The woman in the Punto slowly lowers her forehead to the steering wheel, and the horn lets out an unbroken plaintive wail. The sound renders functional thought impossible, so we decide to skip ahead slightly.

2

"HOW MUCH LONGER MUST we wait for justice?"

This was the last tweet from @naca.zaca before, about two hours later, she was arrested for causing a traffic accident in which one person likely lost their life. "Likely," simply because emergency services have yet to formally update Novi Sad PD of the patient's condition. "How much longer must we wait for justice?"

Although the woman driving the grey Punto hasn't said a word due to shock, the officer inspecting her bag found documents identifying her as "Nataša Žarković," a well-known activist based in Novi Sad with an interest in human rights, particularly those of women, ethnic minorities, and animals, as well as climate change.

"How much longer must we wait for justice?"

The tweet echoes a third time in the head of the inspector on duty as he opens Nataša's file. It is, due to her often creative forms of protest, a hefty folder; photographs and floppy disks threaten to spill out along with numerous criminal charges for public disturbances and official statements she has signed.

STATEMENT

I hereby state that on June 5, 2011, during a protest against the Korona circus, visiting at the intersection of Liberation and Tsar Lazar Boulevards, I did strike the circus owner on the head and back with a wooden placard, thereby causing him minor physical injuries. My intention was to demonstrate the animals' emotional state when their trainers apply physical discipline in the course of training.

Nataša Žarković

Office of the Basic Public Prosecutor

of Novi Sad

CRIMINAL COMPLAINT

Complainant: The People of Novi Sad

Defendant: Nataša Žarković, Executive Director of the Women's Bureau, NGO

Offence Description: Disorderly conduct, disturbing the peace, and obstruction of law enforcement.

Explanation: On May 8, 2013, at a public gathering in front of Novi Sad's Basic Court supporting female victims of sexual violence, Ms. Nataša Žarković removed her upper garments in protest against Mr. Petar Salatić, assistant director of City Greenery, accused of sexually harassing six colleagues. Holding garden shears, she led chants demanding Salati's castration. When police tried to intervene, she insulted them and threatened to remove their fingers if touched. An unidentified individual persuaded her to dress and she left for Radnička Street. The incident was captured both on private mobiles and by Radio-television Vojvodina. The RTV report from that evening is attached to this complaint.

Serbian Ministry of Internal Affairs
Novi Sad Police Department

"How much longer must we wait..."

The door to the inspector's office swings open, and an older uniformed officer storms in, shouting:

"Milonja, it's no use, damn it—she just sits there, staring off into space! I've yelled at her, threatened her, and still nothing. I guess I could try smacking her a few times..."

"No, no!" the inspector interjects before adding, "Let's, ah, wait a bit, and then I'll give the smacking a shot."

The uniformed cop nods. "Do we have the vic's identity?"

"Nope."

"You waiting for word?"

"Not really."

"They say there are no skid marks."

"That's right."

"I knew this madwoman would end up killing someone sooner or later."

"Really?" The inspector raises an eyebrow.

"One hundred percent! I bet you that guy was an investor or a politician, or, like, some corrupt official skimming off the top of public contracts"

"That would make sense. Sure."

The older officer tries to say something more, but his radio cuts him off. After a brief crackle of static, the walkie-talkie whispers fuzzily: "Ković, she's crying."

"Crying?" Ković looks befuddled.

"Crying," the interrogating officer replies. "I don't...know what to do. I feel sorry for her."

Ković slaps his forehead in disbelief, comments on how they'll let anyone into the police force these days, and mutters a curse.

"I'm on my way," he snaps, before flinging himself out of the room as thunderously as he had entered. The inspector continues to flip silently through Nataša's file. Now seems as good a time as any to leave him to it and to learn more about him from the chatter around the police station.

They say Milonja Šoškić might be the finest detective the Novi Sad PD has ever had. He's been married four times, not because he's a great charmer or playboy, but simply because the marriages were, by nature, bigamous—he was already married to the job. In his younger days, he would sleep in his office for nights on end, and come home only to wash, if at all. From the early '90s forward, he'd arrested several of Novi Sad's most prominent—and corrupt—business leaders, often paying the price. Despite penalties and reprimands from his superiors, and resentment from his peers, Inspector Šoškić stuck to his principles and uncompromising pursuit of justice.

Until recently.

Until one Thursday morning, almost a year ago now, when Milonja Šoškić looked at the case file on his desk and decided not to open it. He placed it in his drawer, had a leisurely breakfast, and then played computer solitaire for the remainder of his shift. The cause for this new attitude was much debated in the corridors of the Novi Sad PD central administration building. Was he simply fed up, or had some syndicate found Šoškić's weak spot and turned him at last? The rookies all assumed the latter, but the more seasoned officers, those who had known him since the early days, didn't seriously entertain the notion. "The flame can't burn forever" they would offer sagely, "and Milonja burned brighter and longer than most.."

Inspector Šoškić closes Nataša's file with a sigh. His face wears the unmistakable expression of someone about to do the exact opposite of his heart's desire.

For, in his mind's eye, Milonja Šoškić sees an enormous basket overflowing with a freshly baked loaf of bread, Banja Luka kebabs, chopped onions, and a saucer of homemade yoghurt on the side. In the background glows an inviting hearth. But, instead of an accordion and singing, he hears Nataša cry out:

"How much longer must we wait for justice?"

It's hopeless to throw this file in the drawer, hopeless to cover his ears—the sentence blares inside his skull, a mantra with a life of its own... "How much longer must we wait for justice?"

Šoškić closes his eyes...

"How much longer must we wait—"

He grimaces...

"How much longer—"

The inspector stands, opens his office window, and sticks his head all the way outside. He yearns for the spring air to jolt him awake, for the sounds of the city to drown out the corrupted audio file playing on repeat inside his head.

But it doesn't stop, not until he says aloud:

"How much longer must we wait for justice."

3

WE'VE ALREADY MET POLICE Sergeant Ković. Here he is again in the interview room, scowling silently at a tearful woman from across a table. The young colleague who'd radioed him earlier stands dejected in the corner, avoiding eye contact with either of them. Despite the building's no-smoking policy, the room smells like two decades of cigarette smoke—likely the last time the walls had been painted. The furniture is dilapidated, foam sticking out from the chair cushions. The bleak setting perfectly reflects the expression on Nataša's face.

"Aargh, stop it already!" Ković breaks the silence and admonishes his suspect, but to no avail. Nataša weeps, burying her face in the crook of her elbow. The pose of a hungover barfly before her morning elixir kicks in.

"Don't—" he tries again, speaking more softly. No effect. He spreads his arms, looks helplessly at the ceiling.

"Nataša, cut it out! You haven't killed anyone! I'm. Trying. To. Tell. You..." he says with all the authority he can muster, emphasising each word.

But it's hopeless; the suspect continues to sob inconsolably into her elbow. Ković grabs the sides of his head, clearly driven to the edge of sanity. A parent traumatised by a newborn's endless sleepless nights. He jiggles his right leg and whistles nervously through his teeth. He steels himself for another attempt.

Glancing at his young colleague, Ković realises that this next gambit might tarnish the rookie's image of him...and rookies are known to talk. But he has no other option. He places his hand on her shoulder and, mustering as much gentleness as possible, says:

"Don't cry, Nataša. Everything will be okay."

...

...

To Ković's surprise, she begins to calm down. Her sobs soften into deep breaths, although her head remains on the table. The older cop wipes some sweat performatively from his brow. The gambit worked. Or, it seems to have worked.. Just as a comforting silence settles, however, and Nataša begins to raise her face, "From Ovčar and Kablar" starts blaring tinnily from the rookie's pocket.[1] He scrambles for his phone but—what a klutz!—drops it with a clatter. Nataša bursts back into tears. Ković seethes in exasperation. He fights and then surmounts the powerful urge to administer his colleague a disciplinary slap.

1. Patriotic song referencing two mountains in Serbia, and the bravery of soldiers defending the motherland. Dates from the Partisan resistance against Nazis and collaborators.

"Sorry, mom, I can't talk right now, bye," the young officer says quickly, and then disconnects the call.

"God *damn* it, rookie! Just when I...!"

Ković's colleague may be new to the force, but knows when to keep his mouth shut. A flustered Ković shakes his head, and prepares to try the gentle approach again. He reaches out for Nataša's shoulder but, just a hair's breadth away, "From Ooovčar..." blares out again. Ković stares at his hand for a moment, before slamming it down on the table and cursing as he thunders out the door. The younger officer touches the designation stitched on his navy-blue shirt—"PC 122586"—and retrieves his phone to return the call. He's furious. He shouts at his mother, tells her repeatedly that he cannot talk when he's at work. He'll call her back at 6pm!

The rookie's mother seems to have limited sympathy for his situation, however, and PC 122586 can't bring himself to end the call. He does, however, roll his eyes prodigiously. Although we can't make out her individual words, the message is unmistakable. *So, everyone else is more important than me. You never have time for your mother. I don't ask for a lot, son, just a few words. Is that too much?* After a few minutes of lecturing and unsolicited advice, our rookie feels like a piece of literal shit, and a rather sloppy one at that. He wonders what he could have done to deserve such a miserable day; perhaps some offence against nature in a previous life. Suddenly, Inspector Šoškić materialises at the door. *Great, a third person to disappoint*, thinks the young police constable. Instead though, Milonja pats him benevolently on the shoulder, and gestures to continue his conversation.

The inspector approaches Nataša and whispers something in her ear. This puts an end to her sobbing, which is replaced by a look of baffled alarm. She raises her eyes, her gaze blurry with tears but hearing him clear as a bell.

"Nataša, I believe you're in grave danger. We need to leave, immediately."

"I'm...I'm sorry? What are you talking about, leave? And go where?"

"I don't know."

For the next twenty seconds, not much happens. Nataša and Milonja look at each other. In the background, our PC paces and resignedly accepts his mother's tirade.

If it weren't for the wall clock relentlessly ticking away the seconds, one might think time had stopped. A good film director would surely freeze this frame, we think, scoring it with dramatic strings. The pair seem acutely aware that they are on the cusp of a momentous decision. The minute hand clicks to twelve, and now it's 11pm.

As if waiting for the hour, Milonja grabs Nataša abruptly by the upper arm. He leads her out of the interview room, an officer on his thousandth perp walk. Their pace is hurried, and our PC waves his phone unnoticed as they glide through the door.

"Yes, Mom, I can hear you. I'm here... I'm listening, Mom..."

4

WE START THIS CHAPTER in the same room as we ended the last one—so, what's going on?

As if in reply, our weary PC 122586 gestures haplessly to the wall clock with his phone. The time is 12:22, almost an hour and a half since Inspector Milonja Šoškić and Nataša Žarković took their leave. But, hold on,, that would mean that he's been on the phone with his mother for this entire time...

"I know, Mom, I know. I'll be careful. We've been over this at least ten times now."

Oh, Lord help us!

"All right, Mom, I *promise*... Now, I really have to hang up. I can barely feel my ears. Goodbye, Mom, bye... send my regards to everyone, bye... OK, bye! I love you too. It's no trouble, I love you. That's right. Bye!"

How best to describe a man's psyche after ninety straight minutes on the phone? What remains of our PC more closely resembles a wrung-out rag than a human being. Face pale, lips chapped, ears red. Vacant, thousand-yard stare. The defeated rookie slumps into a chair, and massages his temples. His face contorts in pain, then relaxes after a moment. We can even begin to imagine the faintest hint of a smile...and that's when an energetic Ković bursts back into the interview room, closely followed by two new faces in nondescript suits. The young officer leaps from his chair. He recognizes the two suits before Ković's introduction:

"Kid, these are colleagues from the BIA.[1] Where's Žarković?" PC stammers, eyes wide, like he's just realised that he's walked naked on to Liberation Boulevard, shocking onlookers and spurring the laughter of schoolchildren. A real shock.

The younger of the two BIA agents is huge, so massive that his entrance seems to darken the entire room. We think that a body of this volume likely absorbs some light directly, simply as a matter of physics. In addition to being enormous, the younger agent is visibly irritated. His older colleague isn't nearly as large and, at first glance, lacks the other's irritation as well. He smiles, albeit without warmth, and leisurely surveys the room. But our PC isn't fooled. This grey-haired gentleman in a black raincoat is a dominator, an overlord, whose primary goal in life is to keep anyone around him from getting comfortable. Authority personified. PC's voice sticks in his throat, which leads Ković to break the awkward silence.

"Speak up, kid, you didn't hear me? Žarkovic: where? I left you here with her."

---

1. The Bezbednosno-informativna agencija, "Security-Intelligence Agency." Serbia's national intelligence agency and the institutional successor to Yugoslavia's secret police.

"I... I don't know... she, er, left..."

The older security agent bursts out laughing. His younger colleague soon follows, and Ković joins in with a hesitant chuckle.

"She popped out to walk the dogs, back any minute now, is that right?" the lead intelligence agent jests, continuing to amuse both himself and the rest. Apart from our PC, of course, who stands silent and desolate. He waits anxiously for the laughter to subside so he can finally lance the boil.

The jokes continue unabated, however, waves of laughter breaking over the young cop like high tide at Sutomore Beach.[2] Just as the laughter subsides and the young PC can start to collect his thoughts, the older agent rounds on him furiously. He grabs the rookie by the chin, squeezes, and hisses an inch from his face:

"Spit it out, kid! Where the hell is she?!"

PC mumbles something, and the others lean in to try and decipher his mushy whimper. No luck. The older agent's grip on his mouth makes it impossible to parse any distinct consonants, let alone any words. Several seconds pass before the BIA agent finally accepts that he'll have to ease his grip to hear the PC's report.

"She left with the duty inspector!" the rookie gasps.

"With Šoškić?" asks Ković. The young officer nods in affirmation, adjusting his jaw back into place.

---

2. Vacation destination in Montenegro.

"Šoškić?" the hulking younger agent speaks up. "Who's that, boss?"

"Milonja Šoškić, Gvozdenović! You must have heard of him. The famous Eliot Ness of Novi Sad," the grey-haired agent remarks with a cynical smile. "Ković, call him now, find out where he is."

The older cop grabs his phone, dials, the whole room waits with bated breath...

"He's not picking up. I bet he took her for an impromptu interrogation," Ković suggests.

"I bet he didn't," the older agent replies.

5

A RED 1991 RENAULT 4 idles in a dimly lit dockyard near Štrand.[1] Nataša Žarković and Detective Inspector Milonja Šoškić sit silently in the cabin, staring ahead, thoughts swirling. The situation has clearly grown more precarious since we left them.

"Nataša, did you know that Pešut was a BIA agent?"

"Of course. That's why they're protecting him."

"'They' who? Protecting him how?"

"'They' are the state, of course. He's been formally accused of complicity in a war crime. The slaughter on Borja, near Teslić. Twenty-eight civilians. But the hearings have been postponed again, and again, and again..." Nataša's eyes shimmer with fury.

"So you just, what? Decided to take matters into your own hands?"

"No!" she exclaims, before adding, "Not...exactly. I did want to frighten him. I wanted to remind him that his crimes are not forgotten. That he can never rest easy."

---

1. Famous beach in Novi Sad.

"Did you stop to think about the consequences?" She answers after a brief hesitation:

"I never think about the consequences."

It's said that words can't move mountains, topple houses, or conjure hurricanes to sweep away cities. And, granted, they might not blaze forests or melt glaciers, but their impact can be astonishing. Nataša's words, for example, cause Inspector Šoškić's heart to leap all the way down to his prostate, which throws his entire body off balance. *I never think about the consequences.* Astounding! The phrase is painfully familiar to him: his mother admonished him with it often, as had each of his ex-wives. He itches at the memory. *Milonja, don't you ever think of the consequences?* That's him. He spent his whole life staunchly upholding the law, battling crime and corruption, striving to be good and just. His passenger is an enigma—runs over a BIA agent with her car and then claims never to consider the consequences?

He drums his fingers on the steering wheel, staring forward but stealing glances at his passenger. He decides that, in addition to being enigmatic, she's actually quite beautiful. Her nose is hooked and on the prominent side, while her undyed hair makes her look a good decade older than her age. The glasses she wears have bold frames, which wouldn't look out of place on a university student. Her skin has the greyish tinge of a lifelong smoker, and her lips are tightly pursed to keep her from crying. The two couldn't be more different, but he recognises something in her—to Milonja Šoškić, she is beautiful.

"'I never think about the consequences,'" Milonja says aloud, surprising himself. "That's a sentiment one can hold at seven, eleven, sixteen—at most nineteen—years of age. But when you're..."

"Fifty-seven." Nataša's voice trembles with the stress of the past several hours. "Listen, Šoškić, I've had my fill of one mother. I don't need another. *One can hold that sentiment at seven, at most nineteen...*" She allows herself a smirk and adds, "Besides, no one forced you to help me."

"Wait, Nataša, you don't understand... you don't realise who you've hit, who Pešut is now, rather than thirty years ago. The people he's connected to, and what they could do. If you'd stayed at the station, tomorrow morning could have been very, very bad."

"Oh, please, that's an exaggeration," she says, before adding with another smirk, "I don't know how I've survived without you until now."

"This is serious Nataša! Really serious. How can I—"

"You see, Šoškić," she interrupts, the smirk gone, "my *only* concern right now is that this man doesn't die. Not because I fear some big retaliation, but because I couldn't live with the knowledge that I took a life, anyone's life."

Milonja glimpses a tear sliding down Nataša's cheek, just before she turns away towards the window. He begins to say something but stops himself at the last moment—somewhere around wife number three, he learnt that his verbal ineptitude makes things worse as often as not. He crosses his arms, and uncrosses them. If he hadn't quit eight years ago, he would certainly have lit a cigarette. He tries to think of an excuse to leave the car, but nothing occurs.

Milonja waits, Nataša sniffles, and time crawls. The car radio crackles briefly but, after flipping through three or four radio stations, each blaring some awful music, Milonja gives up and clicks it off. It wasn't the best idea. The Renault's cabin returns to uneasy silence. Some of us suggest taking a break, if only to stroll around the parking lot and give them some space, but the ringing of Milonja's phone interrupts the discussion.

Rather than answer it though, he stares at the screen until the ringtone stops.

"Nataša, I think we're running out of time. That was the station and..."

"Why are you doing this?" The inspector pauses, then:

"I don't know, Nataša... but you'll be the first to know when I figure it out. For now, you need to run home, pack some essentials, and be back here in..." Milonja checks his watch, "Ten minutes."

They look at each other for a moment, the silence heavy. Finally, Nataša leaves the car and disappears into a nearby high-rise. Milonja immediately switches off his phone, and then loses himself in thought. When a quick glance at his watch reveals that eleven minutes have passed, a knot starts to form in his stomach, and he steps out of the car. He paces back and forth behind the bumper, casting a look at the highrise's entrance every three seconds or so. Nothing. Every new glance at his watch takes another bite out of his heart, and the three-second interval narrows to two. Who knows how our tale would have unfolded, had Nataša, at minute thirty-eight, not appeared with three rambunctious dogs and possibly the largest suitcase the inspector has ever seen. Milonja, rooted to the asphalt, doesn't think to offer assistance until she's at the door. Making the sign of the cross, he mutters under his breath:

"What have I gotten myself into? She's completely mad!"

6

It's twilight in a wooded valley. At a long wooden table sit a dozen famished youths hungrily spooning beans into their faces. Sitting among them is a single older man wearing a bowler hat, an olive-green collared shirt, and a deeply confused look behind thick glasses. The Youth Volunteers[1] are wearing the same shirt as he is, although his is soaked in sweat. This explains why no one is sitting near him...however a different mystery continues to vex the older man.

"How the hell did I get here, and who are all these kids?" he wonders.

"Easy there, grandpa, don't overdo it. Remember, you nearly suffocated us with those silent farts the other night," a young man to his left teases, drawing titters from the gallery.

---

1. These are members of a "Youth Work Brigade" (Omladinske Radna Brigada) taking part in a "Youth Work Action" (Omladinska Radne Akcije), organised by the Yugoslav League of Communists. The purpose was to build physical infrastructure, as well as solidarity and patriotism. Youth Work Actions were first organised in Yugoslavia to rebuild after World War II; after a decline in popularity, the practice saw a revival in the late '70s. "Volunteer" is used here instead of the literal translation, "Brigadier" (Brigadir).

Our old Volunteer laughs along, having no riposte. He rides out a few additional jokes at his expense, when the young Volunteers suddenly arise—seemingly finishing their meals in tandem—and leave him at the table. Once he finishes eating, he gets up himself and takes a leisurely stroll down the hill to a small brook. The burbling water makes him desperate for a pee; he scrambles to a nearby patch of trees, and releases his stream just in time. After a few moments, however, he's startled by the giggling of a few women Volunteers watching him from behind the foliage. To the young women's amusement and his chagrin, the blushing old Volunteer fumbles to shield his dignity from their curious eyes. A childhood memory flashes across his mind, from either the first or second grade; he had tried to discreetly pass gas in Serbian class but instead had let out a small, sloppy accident. Not knowing what to do, he pretended that nothing had happened, stared at his notebook, and hoped that the bell would ring soon enough to make his escape. Instead, his nose began to tickle with the whiff of his shame. And he wasn't the only one to notice—everyone around him began to fidget and squirm, some of them pinching their noses. He followed suit, hoping to escape detection. He even joined in with the giggling until the teacher stood up to check everyone's work.

"All right, let's see those notebooks since you're all so restless today!" she declared, moving from desk to desk.

Even as his chest tightened and tears threatened to spill, he continued to play dumb and pointed discreetly at Senada, the

Romani girl in the second row. Hailing from the nearby shantytown, Senada was a useful all-purpose scapegoat for the class.

"My goodness, child, did you have an accident?" the teacher asked him, at full volume, as she leaned over to check his notebook. He met her gaze with tearful eyes and shook his head unconvincingly. She lifted him from the chair, looked down the back of his trousers, and declared, "Indeed, you did!"

As laughter echoed throughout the classroom, he was transfigured into the warm little turd sitting in his pants—an impossible feeling to forget. The scars of public humiliation run deep and heal crudely, always waiting for the right time and place to reopen. A time and place like the Youth Volunteer Action Morava '81.

The old Volunteer hastens to zip his fly, fumbling in his haste, which only delights the girls more. *Stop it, for heaven's sake!* he screams internally, as the tears finally come in force. They trickle around the heavy bags under his eyes, over his cheeks, and down to his trembling bearded chin.

One of the young women Volunteers does eventually notice the tears, and quickly tries to silence the others. She waves frantically, gesturing for them to quiet down, and they leave him alone at last. He begins back to the valley only once his pants have begun to dry from the unfortunate interruption to his stream. Back in the camp, he tries to slip past a group of youths unnoticed; they're sitting in a circle on the ground, one of them playing guitar, while the others sing along.

“Old man, come over here!” he hears a voice call out shrilly. He keeps moving but cannot help glancing over. They’ve all turned towards him, and are staring intently.

“Another time, friends! I have to go... over there!” he gestures vaguely.

“Come on, grandpa, join us! Grandpa! Grandpa! Grandpa!” the same shrill voice begins to chant, and then clap. This encourages the others to join in. The valley soon echoes with, “Grandpa, grandpa!” The joyful youths cheer faster and louder. He feigns reluctance, but he’s clearly started to enjoy the attention. This further energises the Youth Volunteers, and their chanting finally wins him over.

Few can resist the pull of the crowd. They herald him with ovations as if he had organised the Volunteer Action himself. He doesn’t give a speech—nothing to say—but the sudden attention and camaraderie warm him. The assembled Youths begin to pepper him with questions, which he answers with great pleasure (and at some considerable length). Along the way, someone hands him a bottle of rakija[2] and they begin a series of toasts: to labour, to the party, to Tito, to rakija itself.

“To life, grandpa!” the familiar shrill voice shouts, and the toast echoes among the youths.

“To life!” the old Volunteer agrees.

He laughs, lifts the bottle, and takes another swig. The youths' company has made him so content that he's completely

2. Balkan fruit brandy.

unaware of a growing chill in the valley as night begins to fall. With each sip, he becomes more and more sociable...with the opposite effect on the youths, who begin to grow bored. This goes completely unnoticed by the old Volunteer. Inhibitions loosened, he drones on about his achievements in the world of literature, the awards he's won, and those which were stolen from him. He compares his books with those of some Nobel laureates; a poet above all, he also mentions that he dabbles in music. One of the youths, sensing an opportunity to cut the monologue short, urges him to play a song. The old Volunteer makes a show of humility, perhaps hoping for another chorus of "Grandpa!" Nothing like this happens, but a smattering of "Yeah!"s are enough to persuade him. He takes the guitar in his hands and begins to play.

Pling-plonk, guitar strings echo through the camp, and a startled flock of birds erupts skyward from a nearby tree.

Plink-plonk, the circle of youths exchange incredulous glances. *Trinkn-trn*, the instrument seems to cry out for mercy, *drn-drn-trinkn-trn*, and then—regrettably—he begins to sing. The song is so garbled and out of tune that the crowd thins within seconds. However, intoxicated by his song, and also the rakija, he doesn't notice. By the seventh repetition of the chorus, it's clear that he would play and live in this moment forever if he could. But he can't. So instead, he eventually stops mid-stanza. By the end, only four of the most sympathetic audience members remain. Suddenly, the old Volunteer begins laughing hysterically. He takes a few more swigs of rakija, empties the bottle, and collapses face-first on the ground. The remaining youths give his shoulders a shake, but he just grins in his torpor, and mumbles something entirely incomprehensible. They contemplate simply leaving him in the meadow to sleep off his hangover, but a young woman Volunteer speaks up to rouse the others' conscience. Each grabbing a limb, they carry him to his bed. He falls asleep instantly—peaceful as a baby, but snoring like a bear. His sleep is so deep and contented that he might have wet himself in the night had his roommates not shaken him furiously awake. He doesn't immediately understand what's happening. Although the old Volunteer barely feels the blows, a blanket wrapped around his body seems to suffocate him. He struggles to throw the blanket off, drowsy and weak. He needs to pee, his head is throbbing and he's struggling to breathe. At the climax of this desperate fight for life, he lets out a ghastly scream, abruptly sits up, and emerges—from under his coat. At first, he is conscious only of the sun and the pain. Then, it's just the pain.

Voja Počuča shrugs off his coat, grimacing as he rises from the leather armchair. The next few minutes pass in utter numbness, his thoughts somewhere else entirely—perhaps still at the Youth Volunteer Action Morava '81. Behind him, there's a large banner with large stylized Cyrillic letters reading "C-T-C", and below, in smaller font, it says "Club of True Creators."[3] Our somewhat neglected protagonist has evidently spent the night on the premises of this artistic association. On the wall hangs a large framed photograph which features Počuča surrounded by a small group of men. Attached to the frame is a gold plaque engraved "CTC / Founding Assembly / June 25, 2019". These are clearly significant men, intellectuals *par excellence*. Their dignified postures and confident gazes leave no room for alternate interpretations.

Voja Počuča groggily stretches his joints—first the neck, then shoulders, hips, knees, and finally his fingers. He takes out his phone and dials...

"Police?"

"*Yes.*"

"Good day! I'd like to report an attempted murder."

"*Murder?*"

"Yes."

"Someone tried to kill you?"

"*Yes, someone tried to kill me.*"

"When did this happen and what exactly took place?"

Voja begins to recount the event we witnessed earlier, which leads us to wonder if this is that poetic licence we've heard so much about. For, in this version, Rajko Pešut was a passerby

---

3. Uniquely among the world's languages, the Serbian language has long been written in both the Latin and Cyrillic scripts. Although both scripts are used freely by the whole population, the choice to use Cyrillic has at times been associated with Serbian identity and nationalism. The mutually intelligible Bosnian and Croatian use only the Latin script.

who, through simple bad fortune, found himself under the wheels of Nataša Žarković, militant feminist. The actual target was, of course, Voja Počuča himself, who had recently provoked her ire with a comment on Facebook.

"You really think someone would kill you over a Facebook comment?"

"One should never underestimate the power of the written word. Especially the *professionally* written word."

"*And are you a professor?*"

"No, I'm a writer."

"*Alright, Mr...*"

"Počuča. Vojislav Počuča."

"*The suspect is already in custody, and someone will likely be in contact soon to interview you as a witness.*"

"Yes, I presumed she was arrested. However, I slept at an unknown and safe location which, intending no offence, I wouldn't disclose even to you now. Not because I don't trust you, but because this is bigger than all of us. Nataša Žarković is but a tentacle of a monstrous kraken that has been spreading its malevolent influence for years."

Silence...

"*Well, of course, no problem, sir. Goodbye...*"

"Wait, wait, what about protection?"

"*I'm sorry?*"

"They attempted to assassinate me, officer! Don't you think I'm owed protection?"

"*Well, there's a procedure...*"

"Procedure?! Listen here, I'm not just any citizen! I'm a recognized artist, one of the founders of the Club of True Creators, and a figure of significant public interest. I, sir, demand police protection, and forthwith!"

"All right, sir, calm down. Please discuss this with my colleagues when they contact you. They'll be in touch. Goodbye."

"Yes, but when will..."

Voja realises mid-sentence that he's speaking to a void. He further observes that the officer never asked for his phone number or any other contact information. Our protagonist begins to doubt that the police will contact him. Setting his irritation to the side, he sends a Viber message to a four-member group called "Club of True Creators," of which he is the administrator.[4]

Brothers, colleagues, friends, I narrowly escaped an assassination attempt yesterday. I am calling an urgent extraordinary meeting of the Club. I await you at the CTC premises.

A text message follows a minute later, followed by a phone call, then another text, a text, a Facebook message, a text, an email, a text, a text, a phone call... and so it continues for nearly two hours until his phone finally dies from a drained battery.

We owe an eternal debt to literature, which allows us, in a single sentence, to skip over our hero's two-hour orgy of deeply tedious communication with his entire contact book. Over that

---

4. Viber is the most popular messaging app in Serbia. Founded in Israel and owned by a Japanese conglomerate, it is especially popular in Southern Europe, Eastern Europe, and the Middle East.

time, last night's event near the old Jeftinoće Tunnel began to take the shape of a heroic epic.

But let's move on. Around 10:30, a growling stomach carries Voja Počuča briefly outside the Club's premises in search of breakfast. He steps carefully through the door and onto the sidewalk, discreetly observing passersby. Satisfied of his safety, he steps out to a nearby bakery. Head bowed and hands in pockets, he walks with his collar turned up to cover most of his face. Despite his efforts, passersby seem unable to ignore this visibly paranoid man wearing cowboy boots and a bowler hat, probably thinking him an oddball prone to sudden public outbursts. He pauses briefly in front of the bakery window to check for any warning signs inside. Nothing out of the ordinary, except a particularly wrinkled pizza. He enters and orders a burek and yoghurt.

"With meat or cheese?"

"A burek is always with meat."

"For here or to go?"

"To go."

Voja returns to the Club out-of-breath and sweaty, but his face radiates both joy and relief. He devours his breakfast, completely absorbed, and then begins to page through yesterday's still-unread *Večernje Novosti*. On the fifth page, under the crime section, he spots an intriguing headline: "Terrifying! Series of Mysterious Deaths in Novi Sad Continues." Our hero's interest is piqued, but the article is light on factual details. The report concerns the death of a thirty-nine-year-old Novi Sad woman,

Svetlana Simin. Hers is the sixth recent unexplained death in the South Bačka District,[5] and the fourth in the provincial capital itself. As with the previous victims, Svetlana's lifeless body was found with no visible signs of violence. At a news conference, the Novi Sad Police Chief had this to say:

The Novi Sad Police Department is actively investigating the circumstances surrounding the reported deaths. At this juncture, there is no established case, as forensic confirmation determining these incidents as homicides is pending. Preliminary assessments suggest potential suicides, with some indications pointing towards an affiliation between the deceased parties and a dark satanic cult. Nonetheless, the possibility of an unprecedented series of criminal activities in the city's history remains under consideration.

When asked by the *Večernje Novosti* journalist if there might be something supernatural at play in this case, forensic specialist Časlav Trećakov responded:

"In my twenty-three-year career, I've never seen anything like this. I don't know what to tell you. We've sent all our samples to colleagues in Modena, and we're now awaiting analysis."

The writer ends the story on a dramatic note:

Is this once-peaceful Pannonian town transforming into a twilight zone? Has Novi Sad become the European capital of horror? Will this sinister streak of deaths continue and, if so, who will

5. One of seven administrative districts in Vojvodina, and the one in which Novi Sad is located.

be next? Has the devil come to claim his followers...or perhaps everyone else? Soon we will receive answers to these and many other questions. Sooner, I fear, than we expect.

The journalist's effort to unsettle his audience reaches one reader at least, as a wave of anxiety descends on our protagonist. His mouth goes dry, his palms sweat, his chest tightens. His bowels also begin to churn—much, much harder and faster than usual. He gets up and...

Er, honestly, we can probably skip this part without missing anything crucial.

7

In the ICU of the Provincial Hospital, just outside Rajko Pešut's private room, a certain Dr. Besermenji—nicknamed Batman—is talking with two operatives from the Security Intelligence Agency, with whom we are already acquainted. The upper portion of the partition wall is glass, and we can see the patient lying in bed, an IV attached to his arm.

"Well, doctor, what's the prognosis?" the older BIA agent asks.

"It's difficult to know at this stage, and we're still running tests. But I'd say your colleague should be home very soon."

"See, Milovan, I told you!" The older agent smacks the wall in triumph, and beams to his younger colleague. "Pešut is indestructible!"

The doctor continues, "His heart is in great working order. Blood pressure's a bit high, but that's common for his age. His lungs are good, no internal bleeding. He has a small fracture on his left shin and two lesions; one on his head and the other below his right knee."

"Lesions?"

"Swelling, nothing serious. Those should be back to normal within the week."

"Ah, that's great. And when can we see him? We'd love to have a little chat with him, as soon as he's up for it."

"We'll it's...," Dr Batman trails off before starting again, "That's the only thing that might be a problem, you see. At this time."

"I don't follow."

"Well, any conversation with friends and family is likely to unsettle Mr Pešut, possibly very seriously."

"How do you mean, unsettle him? He's conscious, right?"

"Yes, he is conscious, however he's experiencing post-traumatic retrograde amnesia. Dr Babić spoke with the patient this morning, but his memory loss appears virtually complete. He cannot remember his own name."

"Amnesia?"

"Yes. It may be short-term, with memories starting to return in a few days, or the recovery may be rather more prolonged. We'll see."

"Don't worry, doc, it's probably just the short-term thing. In a few days, you won't be able to get him to shut up about his military service. Trust me, if there's anything he remembers, it's that year in Ljubljana."

"It's certainly a possibility, and we're hoping for the best. The duration of amnesia depends on the severity of the injury and the brain's ability to consolidate memories. Consolidation is the mechanism through which temporary changes in neural activity are converted into lasting ones, which allows new synapses to be created between the neurons."

The BIA agents exchange glances. They didn't understand much of that, and are used to despising that which they don't understand. Seeing this on their faces, Dr. Besermenji quickly continues in a more familiar tone:

"The only memory recovered during Dr Babić's assessment was an event from early childhood, involving his grandmother, trying desperately to wake her up. He wept a good bit at that memory, but couldn't remember anything else surrounding it, and no others were recovered.."

The agents look at each other silently. The referee has blown the final whistle, and it's time for the players to exchange courtesies and retire to their respective locker rooms.

Milovan makes the sign of the cross, clearly the more disquieted of the two. His older colleague mutters something to himself. Both then turn to gaze at Pešut through the glass. He's asleep. Moved by the sight of two strongmen at their weakest, the doctor gives both a comforting pat on the shoulder. Intimidating as he is on the outside, Milovan is evidently a more tender soul than we'd realised. Overwhelmed by the sorrow of his colleague and friend's sudden vulnerability, rather than shedding a single manly tear, the hulking agent clenches his fist and delivers a forceful punch to a nearby fire extinguisher. Its dented door flies off its hinges and falls to the ground. Our baffled Dr Batman looks from Milovan to the twisted red metal on the floor, back to Milovan, and then to the older agent. Soon, heads peek from the end of the corridor, nurses and a couple patients drawn by the loud noise. One brave nurse approaches cautiously and asks the doctor if everything is alright. The older agent responds for him:

"Everything's fine, everything's fine. Thank you, nurse, we were just leaving." He grabs the younger agent by the arm and leads him away from the ward at a purposeful yet deliberate pace.

Dr. Besermenji bends down to collect what remains of the fire extinguisher panel, examining it from several angles. As an avid comic book lover and collector, the doctor's first thought is that Milovan must hail from Krypton or some other omni-galactic homeland of superhumans. As he watches them leave, he decides the likeliest theory is that, as a child, Milovan fell into a cauldron of magical potion. "Good lord, doctor! Who was that beast?" the nurse asks, concerned.

He looks at her blankly at first, lost in thought. When he finally comes to his senses, he hands her the red piece of metal and says as he departs:

"A creature from Podbara."[1]

---

1. One of the oldest neighbourhoods in Novi Sad.

8

A RED RENAULT 4 with Novi Sad plates races through the Ibar river valley. It speeds past a sign which reads "Raška: 32 km." Behind the steering wheel is Inspector Milonja Šoškić. Really, he's more on top of the wheel than behind it, as two dogs are panting warmly from the top of his seat back. A third sits on Nataša Žarković's lap, while Nataša herself dozes peacefully in the passenger seat.

On a straight patch of highway, Milonja overtakes a brand new, dark-windowed BMW 7 Series with his shabby red city car. One of us spontaneously comments, "In the hands of Mandušić Vuk, any rifle becomes deadly."[1]

Glancing at the dashboard, Milonja suddenly realises that the car is running perilously out of gas. They'll need to pull over soon, but the inspector clearly isn't rationing gas, his foot resting firmly on the accelerator. He recalls a large Lukoil station from his last time down State Road 22 and, sure enough, a

---

1. That is, "It's not the tool, it's the craftsman." Vuk is a Serbian hero of resistance to the Ottoman Empire, immortalised by Prince-Bishop Petar II Petrović-Njegoš in his epic masterpiece, The Mountain Wreath.

few kilometres before the needle crosses empty, Milonja spots a large service station and pulls up to one of the available pumps. Nataša starts awake and looks around, trying to get her bearings.

"We're near Raška" Milonja says.

"Really? Already? What time is it?"

"It's nine...," he checks his watch, "...fourteen."

"Oh, I'm so stiff, Milonja. Can we get out and grab a coffee?"

"I don't know... We should—"

"I really can't function without my coffee."

"Well... I'm not certain..."

"Come on, Šoškić, ten minutes, ok? Ten minutes won't make any real difference one way or the other."

Milonja relents, sighing. "Fine. Ten minutes. We need to—"

"Great! Could you walk these guys around while I dip out to the loo?"

"Walk... Wait, what?!"

"Just a short walk, over there by the meadow. They'll go quickly enough."

"Wait a minute, Nataša. I've never had a dog. I don't know..."

"Don't know? Don't know what?"

"Well, how it's done."

"You solve complex cases, pursue and bring criminals to justice, and you're telling me that you don't know how to walk a dog? Milonja, really?"

"Also, I need to refuel first."

"All right, all right. So, while you're filling up, just take them out for a second and I'll order us coffees inside. Agreed?"

Milonja is visibly disgruntled, but the time for protest has passed. All three dogs gaze up at him with shimmering black eyes, full of hope and expectation, and he caves in seconds. The inspector fills the tank hastily and lets the dogs out. The largest one, a scruffy, yellow-grey mix that resembles an unevenly inflated dachshund, releases his bowels as soon as he hits the ground. If the ground were any less firm, Milonja would surely sink through it in embarrassment, all the way to the earth's molten core. He looks around frantically, scouting any escape from his predicament. How? Why? No! What now? Torn between his responsibility for the brown mess on the pavement, and a powerful urge to flee the scene of the crime, Milonja panics and opts for the latter.

From the station café, Nataša watches him as he strolls oh-so-casually away from the car and leads the dogs to a relief area behind the gas station. She smiles in benevolent amusement as she sips her coffee. *What a character!* Each dog is pulling him in a different direction, and he seems entirely at a loss. Milonja untangles their leashes awkwardly, and is muttering something to himself. She probably looks a bit odd herself, giggling into her coffee, but she can't help it. Thinking that, in a different age, Inspector Milonja Šoškić could have been a silent film star in Hollywood, Nataša is overcome by an almost forgotten fluttering in her gut. She shifts position, and sobers instantly. She thinks to herself: *No way!*

To avoid any misunderstanding, she repeats, *No. Way!*

After about ten minutes, Milonja approaches the café window, dogs in tow, and tries to spot Nataša's face among the patrons. When they make eye contact, she raises her cup and gestures for him to come inside, but he replies with a pointed nod to his watch. A pantomime duel ensues between the two stubborn fugitives, of which Nataša is the ultimate victor—Milonja gives up when he realises that everyone on Nataša's side of the glass is staring at him as if he's lost his mind.

He turns, irritated, and drags the dogs back to the car, where he finds a large, heavy footprint pressed into the dogshit. Milonja follows the trail of faecal residue on the asphalt and discovers, at the end of it, a heavy guy in a fancy suit scraping his shoe on the curb. Milonja tucks his head outside the man's field of vision, piles the dogs into the Renault 4, and flies into the station café. He plans to down his coffee in a single gulp and drag his companion back to the car by any means necessary.

"Oooh, Šoškić, I'd almost forgotten your face, it's been so long! I'm afraid your coffee's gone cold."

Milonja simply stands by the table, watching her.

"What's going on, why are you standing? Have a seat!"

"As soon as I finish this, Nataša, we're leaving. No discussion."

"All right, all right, just sit down," she says, raising an eyebrow.

"As soon as I finish my coffee?"

"Scout's honour."

Milonja sits, slams the coffee in one go, rises, and heads for the exit. The man in the suit has his face pressed against the Renault's window, and appears to be unleashing a long-winded diatribe at the dogs inside. Milonja turns immediately on his heel, returns to the table, and sits down. Nataša regards him, puzzled. "What's going on, Šoškić? Sudden change of plans?"

"No, I—"

"You're exhausted. Let me drive for a while, you can get some rest."

"No, I mean, sure, but that's not what—"

"How much further to that monastery? What's it called again...?"

"Banjska, we're pretty close. An hour more, I'd say."

"You know, Šoškić, I've never actually been to Kosovo."

"It would be strange if you had."

"Banjska, Banjska... It sounds familiar."

"In little Banjska lived Lord Strahinić, in little Banjska near Kosovo...," Milonja beginsto recite.[2]

"WHO OWNS THE RED RENAULT IN SPOT NUMBER THREE?!"

Now that he's a bit closer, we see that the man in the suit is wearing a heavy gold chain as well, which, along with his shaved head and thick unibrow, rather counterbalances any

2. The opening lines of Banović Strahinja, a classic Serbian epic poem which concerns a knight who rescues his abducted wife from Ottoman raiders.

refining effect the suit might have had. He shouts again in a two-pack-a-day voice:

"Whose goddamn clunker is that in spot number three?!"

The more sensitive and delicate among us instinctively close their eyes; no good can come of this. While Milonja isn't thrilled at his car being called a 'clunker', he manages to swallow his pride and remain silent. Nataša, taking a different approach, calmly raises her hand and says:

"It's ours."

Milonja starts at the admission, questions his sanity once more, and cradles his head between both hands. As the suited man rages up to their table, those of us who didn't close our eyes earlier now use a hand to cover them, peeking through our fingers. We pinch our nostrils with the other—the stench emanating from the man's shoes is truly otherworldly.

"Look at this!" Gesturing to the stubborn faeces remaining on his right shoe, he shouts, "This is genuine Armani! These shoes cost more than that shitty little car of yours!"

"Wait, sir, wait, please slow down. I'm so confused," Nataša earnestly implores, all innocent confusion. "Aren't the shoes the shitty ones? Not the car?"

The man's brain buffers for several seconds, and he says nothing. He's out of his depth now. What kind of question is this? How is he meant to respond? What even is happening? He stammers, rubbing his meaty head.

"Your shoes really are nice, sir, and they fit your whole ensemble so perfectly," Nataša continues in a gentle and amiable tone. "Can they really be that expensive?"

"Seven hundred euro."

"Seven hundred?! Wow..."

"Seven hundred and twenty, actually!"

"For real?" Nataša asks with wide, innocent eyes. "I really need some shoes like this for when spring comes. Look, Šoškić, they're so beautiful!"

Along with Milonja, we look down at the man's shoes. Suede seafoam moccasins with a rhinestone clasp on the front. Although, the right shoe isn't exactly turquoise anymore, more brownish. And fragrant.

"They're...nice," Milonja agrees unconvincingly.

"I think you mean, they *were* nice. And now they're ruined."

"I know! Such a shame," Nataša said, adding, "If you don't mind me asking, what line of work are you in? To wear seven hundred euro Armanis as your walking-around-shoes?"

"Seven hundred and twenty!"

"Right! Seven hundred and twenty."

"And what does it matter? I'm a businessman. Import-export. I own clubs, restaurants. Is that a problem for you? What's your deal, you think you can distract me into forgetting about my shoes?"

"Well, actually, you got me," Nataša says with a sheepish smile. "That's pretty much what I was hoping for."

"Well, tough luck, lady!"

"Well, if there's still a problem then...I guess Inspector Šoškić here will need to arrest you."

"What?!" The two men exclaimed simultaneously. The businessman turns his attention to Milonja, grabs him by the collar, raises his arm and...

9

NO, WE WEREN'T TOO scared of a fight to find out what happened next. But other events demand our attention, as the True Creators have, at long last, assembled in the main room of their clubhouse. Our protagonist, Voja Počuča, rises gracefully from his chair and, after a brief yet dramatic pause, begins to speak.

"Fellow writers, captains of imagination, please allow me first to thank you all for coming to this extraordinary meeting of our Club of True Creators, despite your prior engagements. Most of you know already why I've gathered you here today, and have probably guessed our main agenda as well. However, I must provide a brief retrospective of last night's events, which demanded today's meeting. Yesterday, at around six in the evening, I was—"

"He can *not* be doing the whole story again!" one of us exclaims in anguish, to which the rest of us reply in unison:

"Oh, yes he can!"

Apart from Voja, the Club of True Creators appears to consist of three older men who share a refined if eccentric disposition. We expect to learn that they are, like our protagonist, accomplished artists themselves. Here is a portly man in suspenders, sporting a handlebar moustache and waving a flask. Next is a lanky, angular gentleman in a charcoal suit and black bow tie, puffing on a pipe. And finally, a sweaty, pallid man with greasy hair, sunken cheeks, and dark circles under his eyes. This last one constantly interrupts our Voja with joking barbs that no one finds funny...not even the portly man, who seems well enough in his drink to do so. The bony, suited man nods occasionally, emitting great puffs of smoke with each nod. Although the True Creators are clearly old acquaintances, they seem less than comradely at the moment—the air is thick with jealousy and passive aggression. Things come to a head when Voja, after another unwelcome interjection from the sweaty, greasy-haired man, shouts:

"Enough already, Borojević! Will you *please* let me finish?!" The greasy-haired man jumps, straightens, and mumbles through his remaining teeth:

"What's gotten into you, Vojo? Why so agitated?"

"Agitated?! Do you mock me?! I've just told you that a lunatic tried to assassinate me yesterday, and you ask why I'm agitated!"

"Calm yourself, Vojo, I'm only trying to lighten the mood..."

"Well, I'm in no mood for jokes, Borojević. I'd love to see how you'd react if the shoe was on the other foot. For, were your very life hanging by a thread, I doubt that you would be in a jesting mood!"

The offending party bows his greasy head and raises a hand in apology. Voja nods curtly, but continues with his tale until a muffled giggle from Borojević—

"Out! Now!"

"Excuse me?"

"I said: Get out! See yourself to the exit at once!"

"What right do you—?"

"I mean just what I said, Borojević. You're expelled from the Club. Please leave the premises forthwith."

"Hold on, mate, you can't just..."

"Why not? We only ever accepted you because of your connections."

"Connections?! What are you talking about? Comrades, are you hearing this?"

"Đorđe, you did vouch for him, did you not?" asks Voja, yielding the floor to the tall, elegant man in the bowtie. Đorđe is apparently a deeply reflective man, not given to hasty or unconsidered remarks. Perhaps even too unhasty, we find ourselves thinking after a minute passes. Taking several long draws from his pipe, he looks at the floor... takes another draw... clears his throat... takes a sip of water. Finally, he begins:

"In contemporary Serbian literature, there are few acolytes of absolute truth so authentic and persistent as the bard from Novi Sad, my longtime companion, Vojislav 'Voja' Počuča. An unparalleled writer of prose and verse alike, his resonant words elevate our consciousness to cosmic heights, to other worlds, whence he, with truest emotion, shares his tales and guides the way to a more fulfilled and complete humanity. On the other hand, friends, I couldn't name many artists with such an uninhibited grasp of form and technique, red-blooded stylists whose storytelling enlightens and entertains, whose fantastical narration prepares a feast from the ingredients of our mother tongue, who, like the Big Bang, cracks open the delicate substance of our ephemeral reality. Let us ask: where would we be today, without Borojević's *Providence Peak*, *The Abysm*, and *Faces of the Devil's Children*? Where, I ask again!"

No one dares to answer. A heavy silence fills the room. The True Creators gaze at the floor, patiently awaiting the conclusion to Đorđe's gracious address. He is, naturally, in no rush. Leisurely, he pulls out a pocket watch from his suit vest, briefly checks it, and returns it without any change of expression.

"It pains me, my brothers in art," he says, "that quarrels should arise among us, wasting precious time in addressing the matter at hand. If I recall the inaugural meeting of the Club of True Creators accurately—and please correct me if I'm wrong—we made a unanimous vow that an attack on any one of us, be it verbal or physical, would be taken as an attack on all. All for one, and one for all, gentlemen!"

Voja and Borojević, equally abashed, nod their agreement with heads bowed. Đorđe continues:

"Instead of rallying against our common adversaries and taking decisive action to put their wrongs to right, we find ourselves taking cheap shots at each other for even cheaper satisfaction. Instead of answering our sacred call as True Creators to rise above the morass of mundanity—to resist the forces of imperial subjugation, to battle the mercenaries of NGOs, to expose false artists chasing frivolous European funds and approval, we work at cross-purposes and thereby dilute our power."

The two feuding colleagues look first to each other, and then remorsefully to Đorđe, who raises his voice to fill the clubroom.

"Favoured sons of St Joseph the Hymnographer, most exalted of songwriters,"[1] Đorđe exclaims, "I appeal to your integrity and exalted wisdom. In the spirit of loyal brotherhood and chivalric honour, I beseech you with my most earnest prayer: Bury your hatchets! At once! Let us unite against these mercenaries of imperialism, these Pharisees of political correctness, and tramplers of freedom. These, *these* are our foes as True Creators. There will be time enough to resolve our petty squabbles between us, but the threat is urgent and retreat is not an option. We must defend ourselves, my brothers! All for one, and one for all!" To the surprise of his assembled colleagues, Đorđe pulls an antique revolver from his jacket and gestures to the air.

"Brothers, this battle which has chosen us will not be an easy one! We must be brave, determined, united, and, above all else, resolute. Nothing less will do. So, I ask you, are we brave?!"

"We are, Đorđe... We're brave," Voja and Borojević respond, it has to be said, rather unconvincingly. Undeterred, Đorđe tries again:

---

1. A Greek monk of the 9th century, especially revered in Eastern Orthodox Churches as one of its greatest liturgical poets. (He is also recognized as a Roman Catholic saint.)

"Are we determined?!"

"Yes! We are!" A slightly better response, but still less full-throated than the situation demands. Đorđe pushes further:

"Are we united?!"

"Yes!"

"Are we..." Đorđe starts, briefly losing track of his adjectives, "...unyielding?!"

"YES!" reply the True Creators.

"I ask you, brothers, are we resolute?!

"YESSSSS!"

Ah! Now, this is powerful. Like a Victory Day in Moscow.

"We didn't start this war, gentlemen," Đorđe proclaims, "But we're hardly unprepared for it. We're ready, comrades, and we've been ready for some time. Isn't that right?"

"Yes, it is!"

"For the honour and glory of True Creators!"

"The honour and glory!"

And that's it! Having whipped themselves into an orgiastic fervour, the True Creators ejaculate themselves accordingly from the clubroom. Except...the portly gentleman is still there. He apparently nodded off at some point amidst the feuding and high-flying oratory.

A few minutes later, Borojević comes back through the door. He shakes the shoulders of the straggler and gently slaps his cheeks, but to no avail.

"Moco! Moco, get up, they're waiting for us!"

A contented snore is the portly gentleman's only reply.

"Moco! God *damn*, you're heavy," says Borojević, trying to lift his colleague.

The heftiest Creator mumbles something incoherent; he seems poised to return to his slumber until Borojević tries to take the flask from his hands. This sobers Moca up instantly, and he fixes his just-opened eyes on Borojević with a deep, inscrutable look. His gaze is bulging and bloodshot, and the room fills with a quiet tension. A sense of deep unease crawls up all of our spines—including Borojević's, for whom this doesn't bode particularly well.

"Hey now, Moco, I'm sorry. I didn't mean to... it's just, we need to go..." The portly gentleman appears to have frozen entirely. He simply stares, and stares, and stares...

And then, abruptly, Moca rises from his chair, takes another swig from his flask, and wobbles with surprising speed out of the Club of True Creators.

"Wait, Moco! Wait for me!" Borojević calls out, trailing behind.

10

Approaching the administrative border with Kosovo, Milonja's red Renault is not a particularly relaxed place to be. The only audible sound, aside from the engine's muffled, monotone growl, is the panting of dogs from the back seat. Milonja sits at the wheel, dishevelled, ruffled, and cheeks flushed. A piece of mostly pink and red Kleenex is stuffed inside his left nostril. He looks almost as angry as he is quiet.

Nataša's many attempts to apologise for the recent unpleasantness he encountered seem to have failed. She's silent too, staring blankly, anxiously, at the road ahead.

11

FOR A MOMENT, WE think we took a wrong turn at Albuquerque and waltzed into an amateur adult film, but the mostly-undressed man with a cigar in his mouth looks familiar... Ah yes, it's that older member of the BIA. We haven't learned his name yet....

It's a grim tableau. The agent's angrily stiff member rests in the mouth of a young redheaded woman, her right buttock tattooed with a winged fantasy creature of some sort, her ample bosom squeezed into a bra two sizes too small. God, this guy is hairy! A real animal. You'd never guess it from seeing him clothed, but the man makes an excellent case for the descent of man from ape.

"He could be Suzana Mančić's ex-husband, you know, the drummer from 7 Mladih," an older lady among us cheerfully observes.[1] And jestingly adds, "Gargamel!"

"He does look like the 7 Mladih guy," agrees someone else, before adding "But he's a doppelganger for Knego."

---

1. Our fellow reader is referring to a Serbian singer and later TV personality, and her ex-husband Nebojša Kunić, a drummer in 7 Mladih (7 Youths).

"Who?"

"Andro Knego, the famous basketball player? The Legend of Cibona? Really!"

On the table next to the bed sit a bottle of whiskey, two glasses, a box of Viagra, and a pair of cell phones. The BIA agent wields a tennis racket in his left hand, with which he smacks his companion's butt every time she stops sucking long enough to pick a hair from her mouth. He repeatedly squeezes her breasts hard enough to elicit whimpers of pain. He looks down at her with a glassy expression of inchoate fury and disgust, so we aren't surprised when he ashes his cigar into her hair.

"What the fuck is this, Mima? I'm falling asleep over here! What am I paying you for?"

Although Mima immediately picks up the pace, the brute changes tack, smacking her with the tennis racket and then throwing her roughly over the table. He initially struggles to enter her from behind due to a substantial height difference in Mima's favour. He fumbles for a while, positioning her butt lower, adjusting his angle of entry, and finally shoving his cock at her with all of his might—successful entry.

The BIA ogre clearly likes it rough. A classic sadist. He doesn't simply fuck her, he pulls at her hair, chokes her from behind, shoves fingers into her mouth and nostrils, bites her shoulder, and, of course, slaps her straight on her tattoo. Mima moans all the way through, doing her best to disguise pain as pleasure and likely wondering if this torment could possibly be worth her fee. Notably, none of us react to the tableau before us. We keep quiet and keep watching, sharing Mima's hope that this will all be over soon. A minute passes, then two, then three, and finally the beast's thrusts begin to accelerate. His face pours sweat and flushes red; he moans, ready to pull out and explode all over her back...when, instead, a patriotic Serbian jingle erupts from his phone, syncopated with powerful vibrations. He stops, curses loudly, snatches the phone off the table, and puts it on speaker.

"This had better be important, Gvozdenović!"

"Well," Milovan starts, now second-guessing himself, "I don't know if it's exactly crucial, boss. Did I interrupt something?"

"Speak, Gvozdenović."

"Sorry, I'll call back later."

"No, Milovan, you won't. You said it was important—now speak!"

"Okay, boss, alright... So, we believe that Šoškić and Žarković have left the city."

"You don't say?"

"That's right," Milovan replies, sarcasm flying over his head. "Agent Banjac spotted Šoškić's vehicle at a toll booth near the Kaćka Interchange last night, a little after 2am. They were headed towards Belgrade."

"And? That's it? Damn your incompetence! I knew all this without Banjac's help." The older agent sighs. "You called Trajković, yes?"

"Yes."

"And, what did he say?"

"Nothing."

"What do you mean, 'nothing'?"

"Exactly that," Milovan answers, "Šoškić is clean as a whistle."

"No, no, no!" the older agent yells in exasperation. "That's not possible, Milovan. Everyone has some dirt on them."

"That's what Trajković said."

"Trajković said?! Listen closely, Milovan: I don't give a flying fuck about what Trajković said. OK? If you can't dig any dirt up on Šoškić, then make something up. He's a gambling addict, wifebeater, kiddie-fiddler, whatever, I don't care. What's important is that we have Šoškić on the front page of every tabloid tomorrow morning, got it?"

"The woman too?"

"What do you think, Milovan? Yes, of *course*, the woman too. Both in the same article!"

"You mean...like, puppets of foreign agents, threatening Serbian interests..."

"That's right, Milovan! See, I knew you'd get there."

"...and I guess we could always throw George Soros into the mix..."

"Yes! Perfect! Wouldn't be complete without him..."

"...all right, boss, I'll get on it. I'm, er, sorry again if I interrupted anything."

The older BIA agent ends the call and attempts a few desultory thrusts before giving up. Pulling out, he slumps into a nearby chair and rubs his face roughly with his hands. Poor Mima remains frozen, bent over the table, until he throws two fifty-euro bills next to her body and says:

"Go on, grab your things and go. You're free."

His words echo in her mind. *You're free*. As Mima hurriedly dresses, packs her things, and leaves the agent's apartment, she grieves for her younger self and dreams of freedom.

12

RETURNING TO NOVI SAD, we find that a beautiful, September night has fallen over the city, her residents leaping to escape their homes and apartments. They stroll their familiar pathways, bumping into friends and acquaintances, chatting a bit here and there. They take their dogs out to a nearby park, and enjoy an ice cream or perhaps a quiet drink by the Danube. It's particularly gorgeous tonight, balmy and not a cloud in sight. The streets bustle with people and, above, the large summer terrace of the Waterfront Army Club is packed. The mood is especially ebullient at this table here, where the renowned local actor Slobodan 'Boba' Stojšin is holding court, captivating those assembled with theatre anecdotes and improvised jokes. The whole table is familiar to us, if not necessarily by name. The woman to Stojšin's left looks like a theatre critic, and across from him is the curator of the Museum of Contemporary Art. To the curator's right is that young playwright who won the roundtable award at the Sterija Festival two years ago.[1] Tr, tr, tr...

"Trnavac! Maja!" one of us remembers.

It's a familiar arty crowd. Urban intellectuals, crusading for "common sense"—and thus constantly at odds with the political establishment. Rebels on an endless mission to build a fairer society. Fonts of progressivism, prophets of doom, the eternally unsatisfied, agitators for human rights and other causes... Oh, and inevitably: the Yugonostalgics.

"What an eyesore, damn it! Our city is starting to resemble a literal nightmare," the theatre critic exclaims after her curator friend throws a passing barb at the new mural on Gogoljeva.

"It's awful, right? It honestly doesn't look like anything at all, let alone Gogol! Maybe a local mobster who got high on his own supply, and he's about to get mowed down in the middle of the street. RIP legend!"

"Disastrous."

"Instead of letting Poštić give his rendition of *The Government Inspector* or perhaps *Taras Bulba*,[2] they gave it to some half-baked art student. Horrible!"

The table take escalating turns in sharing their disapproval of the Gogoljeva mural; this eventually becomes a competition to

---

1. The Sterijino pozorje, Serbia's most prestigious literary festival, which confers its illustrious, eponymous award annually. The festival named after 19th century playwright Jovan Sterija Popović.

2. Literary works by Nikolai Gogol, after whom the street in question is named, and whom the mural is nominally meant to celebrate.

list the most egregious testaments to Novi Sad's aesthetic ruin, the group whipping itself into a frenzy—until Maja Trnavac brings up the new monument to King Peter I at, god help us all, Republic Square. Nothing can top that. They sit in silence, trying and evidently failing to digest the irony. Finally, the curator says:

"I'm sure there's even worse yet to come."

As the sudden dip in spirits becomes overwhelming, Slobodan Stojšin resolves to salvage the evening as only he is able. The thespian stands, clears his throat, and begins to recite some lines from an even more renowned son of Novi Sad with a twinkle in his eye:

"In mountain snow, do footprints trace
Their way to the devil's favourite place.
While feigning kindness, he masks his face
To lead us to The Hague's embrace.
The sea laments beyond the shore,
With whispers old, and ways of yore.
Throughout the fortress, Balaž's roar
Will echo proudly forevermore."

Halfway through, Stojšin's friends are already gasping for air, choking on their laughter. He leans back with satisfaction, takes a sip of beer, squints like Šerbedžija,[3] looks to the sky, and spreads out his arms. Applause suddenly and resoundingly erupts throughout the terrace, spreading faster than Covid. Only as the applause crests does the master of stage bow his head, and place his right hand on his chest. This gesture of humility carries the crowd's appreciation into overdrive.

"Bravo, Boba! Bravo!"

With no backstage to retreat to, Boba Stojšin decamps instead to the toilet, waving and shaking the hands of all those he passes. While he empties his bladder blissfully over the urinal, his friends at the table unanimously conclude, wiping away tears, that he is, indeed, a legend. If Boba did not already exist, then one would certainly need to invent him. When the legend returns to the table, however, after a smattering of autographs and selfies, the party has moved on.

Stojšin's three friends are scrolling their phones, communicating on another, digital plane of existence. Realising that he has no choice but to join them, the actor pulls out his own phone and opens Facebook.

After about a minute, before he has the chance to hit mute, an unpleasant guitar cacophony blasts from his phone. The guitar is terribly familiar to us. Oh yes, it's both familiar and terrible in equal measure.

---

3. Rade Šerbedžija, a beloved Croatian actor. In the course of Yugoslavia's breakup, he started a successful international and Hollywood film career, mostly playing villains.

Stojšin jumps to silence the racket, sparing us the more acute symptoms of exposure—three scandalised faces aside. The appalled looks from his friends prompt a shrug of the shoulders, and the actor shrinks slightly. After this brief but distressing interruption, the table returns to its quest for online diversions. Almost half an hour passes before someone speaks again. The curator:

"Damn, Sanja," the curator says, addressing the critic, "Some Hitler Youth type really went after you on Twitter. After you posted about the collaboration with the Croatian National Theater in Rijeka?"

"You saw that, did you? You can't imagine what's been landing in my inbox!"

"It's awful! Did you report them to the police?"

"What good would that do? I just block them, I deal with it all the time."

"I reported one sicko who threatened to impale me. Every day for three weeks," the critic says, adding, "He also sent me a picture of his dick, of course."

"Jesus, how horrifying! And the police?"

"Nothing. Turned out he's just a regular history teacher in Grocka. Upstanding family man. He has a wife and three kids."

"Holy crap..."

"Hold on, when was this? Did they arrest him? Was he tried?" The curator is eager for more details.

"No, no, I dropped the charges. He sent me a DM with his whole life's story, apologising desperately and begging me for forgiveness. It felt totally pointless..."

"You're kidding," says the curator, nonplussed. Maja and Stojšin tilt their heads, equally surprised.

"Come on guys, what do I gain if this guy goes to jail for two months?"

"Well, I don't know," the curator answers, "You might feel a little bit happier knowing that you at least got one psycho behind bars."

"And even if it's just temporary," Stojšin adds, "having that creep locked away would improve the community's quality of life for those two months!"

"Maybe," Sanja throws up her hands, "Or maybe, after two months, he'd get released and actually, honest-to-God impale me because I had completely destroyed his life." The curator and Stojšin protest:

"Come on..."

"Okay, okay, fair: My friends would defend me, and he very probably wouldn't do it. But surely you can understand that I simply don't *want* to ruin someone's life, even that of a psycho."

Sanja's curator friend, thrown off balance, grasps his head in exasperation. He turns to Stojšin, who shrugs, equally unsympathetic. But Maja, taking the theatre critic's hand, says:

"I totally get you, Sanja. I would've done the same."

"Hold on guys," Sanja starts, "Maybe I'm looking at it wrong, but— "

A waiter suddenly materialises at the curator's elbow. "Sorry to interrupt, ladies and gentlemen, but we're closing the till. I'll need to close you out now."

Everyone reaches for their wallets but Stojšin, beaming beneficently, waves them off. It's his treat—he's just landed the lead role in a new project. His friends' many protests fall on deaf ears, he simply Will Not Have It, and three wallets return to their purses and pockets.

"How much?" he asks the waiter.

"Two thousand three hundred twenty."

"Twenty, you say? Ah, where did that twenty come from?" The waiter shrugs and gazes patiently down at Stojšin. The actor fumbles in his wallet for a few moments, mutters to himself, pulls out twenty dinars, looks carefully at where those bills came from, and then hunts in some additional pockets. He pauses thoughtfully; an unforeseen complication has arisen.

"Damn, where's my money?" he asks no one in particular.

While his friends' wallets resurface to split the bill, Stojšin searches his own billfold frantically, before sighing and shaking his head in resignation. His wife seems to have taken his money. He apologises sincerely to his friends on her behalf, sufficiently distraught to curse his own mother-in-law.

"Damn that crazy bat's old soul!" he exclaims in torment.

The others do their best to console him, earnestly promising that, next time, of course, Stojšin can cover the bill. Only after this promise is made does the actor's mood begin to lighten. A moral discussion follows, concerning topics of forgiveness, societal responsibility, the value of punishment, and whether a person can ever truly change. This goes on for a while.

Finally, the party realise that they are the only remaining patrons. Hostile looks from the waitstaff clearly communicate a desire for them to leave. The four of them look to their watches in unison, and conclude that time simply flies in good and engaging company.

By this point, it's almost certainly too late to expect any goodwill from the waiters. For Boba Stojšin and his friends, who wave innocently and wish the waitstaff a good night, there's not even a pretence of a smile, or even a grunt of acknowledgement. All that remains is highly distilled contempt. But this group is immune to the waiters' hostility, finding it rather amusing instead. Leaving the terrace, they say their goodbyes. Maja tells them she lives just a hundred metres away on Dušana Vasiljeva and, of course, can walk herself home. The rest wave, kiss cheeks, and head in the opposite direction.

Now this is a dilemma, we find. Looking left, then looking right. Who do we follow? They're all only getting further away, and the chapter will simply end if we don't...

"Let's follow Maja!" someone shouts, just in the nick of time, "She's alone after all, and the least we can do is escort her home, since it's so late and her street is, like, eerily dark." And it is. Very eerie, very dark.

So now we're hurrying after her, hoping to catch up. And there she is!

At an earlier hour, if there were passersby in the street, she'd be self-conscious, smiling as she is at the memory of Stojšin's recitation. As it is, she walks with an upright, confident gait, which wobbles slightly only as a sneezy tickle begins to develop in her nose. And then, all of a sudden, she can't contain herself anymore. An urgent rush of air blasts from her nose, carrying with it a big yellow glob of snot, which Maja instinctively catches with her fingers. Moving to retrieve a tissue from her bag, she looks around for any witnesses to her slimy embarrassment.

She glimpses a pair of men's shoes in the shadow of the withering linden tree. Her heart skips a beat. A chill runs down her spine. Uneasy and afraid as she is, Maja can't help but wonder what kind of person is wearing these steel-toed cowboy boots.

"'There are smiles that are worse than tears,' says the great Turgenev." Voja Počuča steps out from the shadows, while his stately colleague Đorđe from the Club of True Creators adds:

"Good evening, Miss Trnavac."

"Who are you? What do you want from me?" Maja asks, staving off panic.

"Who are we? Really, Đorđe, who are we? Who. Are. We!" exclaims Voja with incredulity. "Nothing, perhaps, but the humble foundation upon whose creativity this city's literature is built. Yes, rest assured, you poor little nothing, that the Athens of Serbia would shine less brightly without the polished rhymes of this gentleman right here, the most gallant of Serbian poets, Đorđe Smolović."

"It's painfully obvious," Đorđe rejoins, "And hence unsuccessful, this clumsy attempt to belittle and insult our persons by affecting not to recognize us."

"You're both mad!" Maja cries, now more confused than terrified. "I'm genuinely not acquainted with either of you."

The True Creators exchange incredulous glances at this absurdity. Đorđe pulls out his revolver and says:

"Well, in that case, we insist that you come with us. It's high time we get acquainted."

Maja looks at them fearfully, trying to comprehend a life where comedy can turn to tragedy in an instant. She turns to scramble for her apartment...

The scream never makes it past the doorstep, muffled by a nylon bag that Voja has just thrown over Maja's head. The playwright wrestles fiercely, flailing her arms in resistance, as the True Creators drag her towards a car parked on the street. She's eventually piled into the back seat, next to a deeply-snoring Moca. Počuča leans in after her, doing his best to restrain her struggling hands with duct tape. Đorđe jumps in from the front to assist, and they finally succeed in subduing her. Borojević, at the wheel, starts the car and asks:

"So. Where am I driving to?" Voja replies:

"Banstol, near Fruška Gora.[4] We're going to my cottage."

As Voja directs his sweaty chauffeur, we detect a distinct note of pleasure in his voice. That satisfaction is a beautiful contrast

---

4. A mountain near Novi Sad, known for its natural beauty.

for the yellow bit of slime which dangles lazily from his left earlobe.

13

"ABBOT... ABBOT..." WHISPER TWO clean shaven monks, timidly shaking their superior by the shoulders. The abbot, lost deeply in slumber, mumbles incoherently in reply. He groans, perhaps still dreaming, or perhaps simply annoyed; whatever the case, the abbot is clearly expending great effort to lift his weary eyelids.

His efforts, unfortunately, do not translate to results. The novices would already have given up, were it not for the front doorbell's unignorably persistent clanging.

"Someone's ringing to get in, Father!" they try a bit louder. "Father Stefan, wake up! Father Stefan!" Any louder and they'd be screaming at him.

It is likely that no one among us has had the opportunity to witness the reluctant awakening of an Orthodox priest, and this, we now realise, has been very much our own loss—it's one of those moments to be remembered for a lifetime, like skydiving. As has been said, laughter follows most readily when we try to hold it back.

Abbot Stefan finally props himself up on his elbows, attempting squintily to get his bearings. A stray lock of grey hair escapes the yellow sleeping cap on his head, defying gravity. He smacks his lips, a portrait of confusion and vulnerability. His teeth float beside him in a glass of water, and there's a deep pillow-crease etched into his left cheek. "Someone's at the gate, Father."

The abbot stares at them blankly, the identity of the two monks, and indeed his own identity, an evident mystery to him. Still, he rises from his bed and shuffles half-asleep across the courtyard to answer the banging at the gate. It's probably the same group of youths from the village as always, making trouble in their boredom. Abbot Stefan castigates himself for always falling for it, acting precisely as his antagonists expect.

Abbot Stefan has spent the past three decades in devoted service to God. Through deep and scholarly theological inquiry, he has elevated his inherently sinful human nature. And, through vigilant prayer, he has refined his spirit, transcended many of the greatest human frailties and shortcomings. Unfortunately however, the power to transcend morning grumpiness rests on a higher rung of spiritual enlightenment. At least at this hour of the day. The abbot slips a slipper off his foot and wields it over his head, ready for any comers.

"GO HOME, YOU LITTLE...," he starts with a roar as he flings the gate open. But then freezes upon seeing Milonja Šoškić.

"Easy there with that slipper, Stevo, we come in peace," Milonja jests, "Please be cautious with your weapons of mass destruction."

Abbot Stefan, still a bit stupefied but now wide awake, beams with happiness. He crosses himself, approaches slowly to savour the moment, and finally embraces Milonja so affectionately that we find ourselves similarly engulfed by a feeling of warmth and safety.

"Milonja! What a surprise—I can't believe you're here!" the abbot says, deeply moved. He has so much more that he wants to say, but he holds back to still his quavering voice, and instead rubs Milonja endlessly on the back.

"I'm sorry for not telling you, Stevo, I genuinely did not have the time," the police inspector apologises, adding that he'll tell his friend everything in the morning.

Abbot Stefan vigorously waves away his friend's explanation and then glances at Nataša, currently standing awkwardly to the side. The dogs at her feet look at the embracing men with bewilderment; Nataša's human confusion is only slightly more muted.

"Don't tell me you got married for the fifth time and didn't call me to be your best man!"

A howling wind momentarily carries away all the unspoken words. Several long, dull seconds pass, followed by a few more, then more and more... Suddenly, all of Milonja's discomfort and accumulated shame try to escape through his face. Even in the darkness, we see that his complexion has flushed the colour of a fine Pro Corde.[1] Nataša, perhaps in a noble attempt to break

---

1. A Montenegrin variety of red wine.

the tension and alleviate Milonja's discomfort, begins to emit odd noises—laughter, perhaps, or else maybe a sudden bout of madness. Abbot Stefan, baffled, regards their reactions with concern that the last sane man in Serbia has finally lost it. If the temperature of awkwardness were measurable on a thermometer, it would certainly read at least minus fifteen degrees Celsius. The abbot invites them inside to escape this icy discomfort, shouting for his two novices to bring some food to the dining room and take care of the dogs. In the meantime, he escorts them to their lodgings—a room with several pious icons on the wall, and two small twin beds. Abbot Stefan's eyes twinkle; he hesitates, but then can't help himself:

"I hope you don't mind the separate beds. The monastery's honeymoon suite is under renovation..."

Milonja had just finished off his water bottle, to the abbot's good fortune—otherwise, we would certainly be looking at either a gasping, coughing police detective, or a very wet Orthodox priest.

"Spare me your jokes, Stevo, for the love of God," Milonja mutters, and looks nervously to Nataša. Their eyes meet, flinching at first and then smiling shyly, like schoolchildren with a mutual crush.

14

ALTHOUGH IT'S WELL PAST midnight at the foot of Fruška Gora, Voja Počuča's cottage might as well be in a different time zone for three of True Creators—Počuča, Smolović, and Borojević—with only Momčilović dozing peacefully back in the car. The three éminences grises of Serbian literature sit around the dining table, opposite Maja Trnavac, who is bound to her own chair with several layers of duct tape. In the absence of a table lamp, they have placed a floor lamp with a gaudy shade next to their captive, casting a dim light on her face. An interrogation appears imminent. Đorđe calmly fills his pipe and poses the first question with a tone which is both even and a bit cynical:

"Tell us, Miss Trnavac, do you know why you're here?"

"No idea! May I ask questions as well? If so, why the hell *am* I here?"

"If I may, Maja," he begins, "I'd like to offer you some friendly advice: You are not in a position to be hostile towards us, and it would be unwise to attempt any provocation." Maja successfully keeps her eyes from rolling to the back of her head.

Đorđe sets his revolver down on the table and continues, "You can drop this affectation of surprised naïveté now, you know. You are entirely aware of those whom you've slandered in your writings, those whose dignity and moral credibility you have thrown into question."

"Okay, it's true that I know what I've written. But I don't see how that involves you, any of you. I genuinely don't know who you lot are, and I cannot think of any reason I would attack you. I must be missing something."

"YOU LIE!" Voja leaps from his chair, and reaches for his gun, but a sharp look from Đorđe, and a firm grip on the wrist, hold him at bay. Our protagonist takes a moment to collect himself, then starts again:

"Do you even know, you pitiful creature, what true creation is? Authentic artistic value? You cannot, for, if you did, you would certainly recognize us."

"I think...," Maja hesitates, visibly straining her long term memory, "I think that I saw this gentleman a few years ago on Velja Pavlović's show." Maja gestures at Borojević, who, flustered, is interrupted by an increasingly imperious Đorđe.

"Miss, although I don't value awards greatly myself," Đorđe begins, "I am astonished that someone who claims to be well-versed in contemporary literature is unaware that she is in the presence of winners of virtually every major literary award in Serbia. From the November Citation of the City of Novi Sad, the Simo Matavulj Prize, the Vojvodina Writers' Association Book of the Year, the Spark of Culture Award, to the

Freedom of the Town of Sremski Karlovci, the Vuk Award, the Zmaj Award, Miodrag Dukić Award, the Teodor Pavlović Award and—what else, Boro?—ah, yes, the Slavko Jungić Jesej Award, Đura Jakšić Award, the Honour of the Kosovo Maiden Prize, Mother Angelina of Serbia Award, as well as many, many others. I won't list them all now."

"My publisher recently awarded me for the authentic voice of my prose," Počuča tosses in casually.

"All right, fellas: kudos!" Maja replies. "Consider me genuinely impressed. But I still don't get what it is you want from me. Unlike yourselves, I've received just the one award."

Đorđe pulls a newspaper clipping from his coat pocket and reads aloud:

"'*If until now I wrote plays about social issues, I realised here that true activist theatre has an entirely different character. The beating heart of such work lies not in its topic or aesthetics, but rather the impact a performance has on society.*' Are you familiar with those words, Miss Trnavac?"

"Yes, of course. I wrote them. But surely you're not telling me that this abduction is about literary principles, are you?"

"*Abduction?*" Đorđe shakes his head in disappointment. "Slow down now, Maja, slow down. To start, for me and my fellow True Creators, literary principles truly do constitute the quintessence of the human condition. And we are indeed ready to defend our work and our principles to the death. But this is not the only reason for which we invited you to my colleague's cottage for a friendly chat."

"Excuse me? A friendly chat? Is this how you'd characterise this whole...situation?"

"Well, perhaps not," Đorđe concedes. "We do, however, share an Artist's sense of humour."

The Club of True Creators briefly transforms into the Club of Truly Cracking Up, breaking into uncontrollable laughter. Maja continues to balance terror, irritation, and her own less mirthful sense of the absurd. The three writers eventually settle when Đorđe produces another clipping. He reads:

"*Let's be honest: it was one of the most culturally vibrant, and naturally beautiful countries in the world! Combined with its transnational, non-aligned, and left-wing stance, it's easy to argue that it was, in fact, the best country in the world. Now that it's gone, I realise that it was impossibly utopian and ahead of its time. But as a current citizen of a banana republic, it gives me hope for our future to know that it once existed.*"

"So, it is about politics. I knew it."

"No, no, you're jumping to conclusions again, miss," Đorđe replies. "There's more. Although I must acknowledge that your perspective is inherently hostile and dangerous. Subversive."

Borojević seizes the opportunity to enter the debate: "What do you, poor soul, even know about Yugoslavia? You weren't even born yet when it all fell apart!"

"I was."

"Were you? How time flies," Borojević remarks, slicking back his greasy hair. "But still, you were so young that you have no real first-hand experience, and so your thoughts on the matter amount to an uninformed screed. Take note, young lady: Yugoslavia was the greatest mistake in our entire history! From Grand Prince Župan Nemanja[1] to today. And as for what you wrote about his monument...don't get me started!"

"Ah now I understand: You're an immortal highlander, living from the dawn of Serbian history until now, knowing everything firsthand."

Borojević flushes red. "Listen, kid, don't get cheeky!"

"But gentlemen, do you not, as intellectuals, and, I'm sure, master artists, find it suspicious how spotless our nation's history is? Impeccable. At school, they teach us that we have always been honest, beautiful, just, peaceful, and clever, while the rest of world's peoples—occasionally excepting the Russians or the Chinese—are deceitful, ugly, hypocritical, aggressive..."

"And that's because it's true!" Borojević exclaims. "Young lady, the only blemish on our motherland's face is that misguided union. And even in that case! It wasn't a Serbian idea, and no one ever asked us. The 'great powers' had already made their decision."

---

1. Founder of mediaeval Serbia's most prominent ruling dynasty; his son Stefan the First-Crowned was the first Serbian ruler to use the title of "King."

"Now, to be fair, Boro," Voja interrupts. "it's not as though King Alexander wasn't behind unification. He was pretty Ser bian."[2]

"No, Voja, no! They blackmailed him! Have you even read *Faces of the Devil's Children*? You've had eleven years to read it."

"I...Yes, I have. Of course."

"You obviously have not! If you had, then you'd know that British intelligence blackmailed the Karađorđevićs[3] and forced us into that unholy Franken-state." Voja digs his heels in:

"OK, OK, I haven't read it—but that's only because it's garbage!"

"You dare say that, Vojo!? You, who would not even have published a single book, had Đorđe not arranged your funding at the provincial poetry competition!?" Voja's face darkens:

"What did you say!?"

"You heard me!"

"You Montenegrin piece of shit, I'll make you eat your words!"

Chaos ensues. Đorđe attempts to separate his quarrelling colleagues—now fully at each other's throats—but fails. In-

---

2. King Alexander I, also called "Alexander the Unifier," inherited the united Kingdom of the Serbs, Croats and Slovenes from his father Peter I in 1921. In 1929, he reorganised the state to be more centralised under Serbian dominance and renamed it "Yugoslavia" (literally "South Slav Land"). The subsequent Socialist Federal Republic of Yugoslavia was less centralised.

3. Ruling dynasty of Serbia which produced King Peter I and his son King Alexander I, with its origins in the struggle against Ottoman control in the early 19th century.

stead, he takes an accidental blow to the head and falls to the floor, which in turn knocks over the floor lamp, and plunges the room into darkness. Maja screams. Voja and Borojević continue to fight and curse each other's immortal souls. Dogs bark in the background. A single gunshot cracks at a murderous volume. After that...silence.

15

After their morning exercise, in the garden of the SMEČ[1] tennis club, two older gentlemen sit, wearing white polo shirts damp with sweat, draped in towels. They chat with each other, flip through their newspapers, sip espressos, and eat croissants with Montenegrin prosciutto. We recognise one of them at a distance due to his extraordinary hairiness, while the other is familiar only when we've gotten a bit closer. Unlike the senior BIA agent, though, this other fellow is a public figure—we all recognize him, a politician with boundless coalition options, always in the right place at the right time. He somehow has the time to serve as both the director of a water supply company and the Novi Sad secretary for education. Over the past twenty-five years, he's changed political parties six times.

"You're improving, Opalić," says the hairy BIA agent. "Give it a year or two, and you might even win a whole set against me!"

Some people find defeat hard to swallow. They try to forget their losses as quickly as possible and prefer not to be reminded

---

1. "SMASH!"

of them—especially by the victor. Opalić is definitely such a person. Although he forces a smile, there's an iciness behind his eyes that seems to say: *Keep talking, you idiot, I'll beat you if it's the last thing I do.*

"Hey now," Opalić chides, "I come here to have some fun, get my heart going, not to die chasing every ball like my life depends on it, like you."

"Right, of course," the hairy BIA agent replies sarcastically, "My friend, you're all scraped up from diving on the clay court."

"Come on! I only do that for the laughs."

"For the laughs?" Opalić's opponent laughs himself, amiably enough but devoid of any warmth. "I suppose you also smash rackets after missing a shot 'for the laughs'? And take tennis lessons every Sunday 'for the laughs'? Maybe you should find some guru-coach, like Djokovic had Imaz, to come watch us play."[2]

Opalić takes an enormous bite of his food to avoid having to reply, gulps espresso to wash it down, and begins reading a newspaper article aloud:

"'*Betrayal! Yesterday, Milonja Šoškić, an inspector from the Novi Sad Police Department, assisted Nataša Žarković, a long-time fellow traveller of anti-Serbian interests, in her escape from custody. Just hours before, Ms. Žarković was arrested for the attempted assassination of a high-profile individual, whose*

2. Pepe Imaz, a professional tennis player from Spain, who coached Serbian tennis ace Novak Djokovic through a difficult career spell. His coaching is known for having a philosophical and spiritual dimension.

identity remains undisclosed due to concerns for their safety. The police are conducting an intensive search for the fugitives and urge citizens to report any information to the nearest police station or dial 192.[3] *The Ministry of Internal Affairs has released an additional warning that these individuals are to be presumed armed and highly dangerous. They urge citizens not to approach or confront the terrorists, no matter how deeply their wounded patriotic feelings may drive them.*' Damn, where did they find these photos?" Opalić chuckles. "They look like thugs. Or like...Hannibal Lecter."

"Hmm? Oh yeah I suppose. Wait until you see yours."

The agent's remark cuts Opalić somewhere just beneath his fourth rib. Unsettled, the politician takes a sip of coffee, then another, and would have taken a third had the second not emptied his cup. He regards his friend, blithely paging through his own tabloid, and says:

"Well, my affairs aside, this whole thing stands to turn into a big mess."

"Nonsense," the agent scoffs. "They're both just fools. Zealots. We'll catch them in a few days and that'll be the end of it."

"Really? I love your confidence," Opalić says sceptically. "But if you think about it, nowadays, it's precisely the fools and zealots who pose the greatest threat."

---

3. Serbia's emergency telephone number, equivalent to 999 (UK) or 911 (US).

"Come on! And where did you get that idea?"

"Where? Just think about it."

"Fine, I've thought about it."

"And?"

"And zealots are zealots. Fools are fools. And that Šoškić, he's the Fool Supreme! A worn-out loser in a Renault 4." The politician can't help himself:

"Now now, the Renault 4 is a timeless classic."

"Oh, Opalić, cut the wise cracks! Do you have a point in all of this?"

"Just...be careful. Don't underestimate them."

"Wait, wait, wait." The earlier coldness in the agent's eyes reaches absolute zero. "Do you really think I need your advice? I'll tear them apart! I'll have them for breakfast!"

"All right, all right. Calm down."

For the next few minutes, all we can hear is the sound of croissants being chewed and pages being turned. The tension between the friends becomes so thick, one could not only cut it, but even smell it. Our noses itch, and even our eyes begin to water. Although we soon realise that the likeliest cause is a discreetly-released prosciutto fart, Opalić himself is obviously finding it difficult to handle. His breaths grow shallow and his leg starts to twitch. He glances at his Raymond Weil watch and asks, suffering and stuttering:

"Whose turn is it to pay today? I've got an appointment up on Tzar Lazar Boulevard."

"I've got it," the agent replies. "Grab the waitress on your way out?"

"All right. See you day after tomorrow then."

"Yes, yes, take care."

The agent carries on aimlessly scanning the papers. A text message brings him abruptly to attention—and he clearly did not appreciate the message's content. He crumples his newspaper, tosses it furiously on the table, and storms out of the SMEČ tennis club.

16

"AND SO, STEVO, THAT'S how we ended up here with you."

Having already lived through most of Milonja's tale, this seems an opportune moment to have arrived back at the Banjska Monastery. It's a gorgeous day, sunny and warm, ideal for a ramble; the landscape is breathtaking, and the scent of wildflowers clears away any lingering stench from the previous chapter. Nataša leads the procession with her dogs, followed only by Milonja and Abbot Stefan. She's mildly annoyed by the two men constantly lagging behind, wrapped up in conversation.

"Oh, Mile, my brother!" cries the abbot. "How truly terrible, I'm so sorry. Could hardly be any worse, honestly. Do you...know what you're going to do?"

Some men are open books; Milonja is not such a man. He shrugs passively, cogs almost visibly turning in his mind, but remains silent. Abbot Stefan gathers himself and says warmly, "Milonja, you can stay as long as you like. As far as I'm concerned, you can stay here until the end of time." Milonja hugs his friend.

"We won't need to, Stevo. Two or three days at most. But thank you."

"Two or three days?! You're mental! Where are you going next?"

"I'm not sure yet. We'll see."

"There's no 'we'll see' about it, Mile! You're safe here."

"We'll see, Stevan, we'll see."

Abbot Stefan makes the sign of the cross and begins muttering, apparently to himself. We suspect—and fervently hope—that it's an impromptu prayer, rather than simply an overheated priest. In the meantime, Nataša has taken a seat on a wooden bench. She lights a cigarette, and waits for the others to catch up. She's beginning to daydream when Abbot Stefan calls out, still several paces behind, "Do you know, my dear, how long the two of us have known each other?"

She would essentially need to shout to reply verbally. Not in the mood, she shakes her head instead.

"He hasn't told you?"

As they're still far behind, Nataša's head continues to shake.

"You know what? That's even better! I'll tell you everything, once we've all sat down."

As Abbot Stefan prepares to unleash what looks to be a lengthy tale, Milonja whispers in his friend's ear. Beneath his thick, grey-black beard, a mischievous smile appears on the priest's lips. He pats Milonja reassuringly on the shoulder and begins:

"Well, it was like this: It was eighty..."

"Eighty-two," Milonja interjects.

"Eighty-two, precisely. Idoli had just released their first album,[1] and we were a year from graduation. The perfect soundtrack for the times. Thinking back, it was a wild time. The sorrow for Marshal Tito had faded at last and we were ready to *live*... Anyway, when this tall, handsome, well-coiffed man showed up in our class on September 1st 1982, a commotion naturally ensued. All of us watched him closely while he tried to sneak his way into an empty desk at the back of the room. I don't think anyone even approached you for the first two weeks—am I crazy?"

"Maybe even three," Milonja says with a repressed smile.

"Typical Novi Sad hospitality," the abbot chuckles. "We treated Milonja like he didn't exist but, in reality, we were all obsessed with him. That one kid, Kontara, the mayor's son, was even trying to fight him. They'd barely exchanged two words between them, but Kontara was jealous because he had a crush on Staša in Section 3, and she'd told her friends that Mile was cute. By the way, did you know Staša passed away last year, God rest her soul?"

Milonja nods simply. Glancing over at Nataša, he sees that she is entirely lost in her own thoughts.

"I find out about these things on Facebook," Abbot Stefan adds, before continuing with his story at some considerable length.

---

1. Very popular Serbian post-punk band.

Whether we want to or not, this is how we ultimately learn the bulk of Milonja's life story. That his father had been a major in the Yugoslav People's Army, that he'd been transferred from Kraljevo to Novi Sad and brought his wife and kids with him. That Milonja had pursued criminology at his father's insistence, even though his dream had been to study films, and then make them. Thanks to his father, he'd had free access to the cinema at the Army Club, and he virtually lived there. Stefan, the abbot of Banjska Monastery, was known as Stevan before his monastic life, and his surname was Stokin. The pair became best friends during a senior class trip to Croatia in '83, when Milonja saved Stevan from a serious beating.

The future priest, after consuming too much dingač,[2] had catcalled some girls on the terrace of the Ambassador Hotel. As it turned out, these girls were themselves on a senior trip from Macedonia, and they complained to three of their male friends who resolved to teach Stevan a lesson. This is the point of the story at which Milonja reveals a theretofore concealed knowledge of judo.

We also learn that the pair remained friends throughout their university years, forming a rock band named Protagonisti which had met with moderate success. Most notably, they had opened for Tony Montana at Mašinac, and, after their performance, Tony had gone out of his way to congratulate them on "the most original performance he'd encountered in years." Stevan's

---

2. A fine Croatian red wine.

father was a prominent party leader in Vojvodina, and had sent his son to study economics. He found the field unbearably tedious, finally completing his studies mere weeks before the war began in Croatia. Instead of joining Naftagas,[3] where a job had awaited him for years, Stevan was forced to escape conscription down the road at the Kovilj monastery. And there's more! We also learn that—

"Enough, enough! I beg you to stop!" Nataša suddenly cries out. We all freeze, even the dogs, waiting for some elaboration...

"I really can't listen to this right now, gentlemen. I keep thinking about... Milonja, can you please call someone to find out what happened to Rajko Pešut?"

Milonja hesitates before answering, "I'm not sure...we'd need to be careful, get a local phone number. Stevo, the newsstands must sell SIM cards, right?"

"Probably. And they'll definitely have them at the hotel."

Nataša gets up, whistles to her dogs, and briskly starts back to the monastery. The two friends trip over themselves to catch up to her, or at least follow close behind. As for us... we soon give up the chase, which leaves us wondering what we might have missed in other, less picturesque environs.

---

3. Yugoslavia's publicly owned oil and gas utility.

17

THE MID-MORNING SUN ONLY partially breaks through the blinds in Voja's Fruška Gora cottage. Maja Trnavac, flecked with escaped rays of light, is seated in a rather awkward position. Alarmingly still. Still taped to the chair, her head hangs limply, and there's something dangling from her chin. In this dim light, it's hard to make out what this is, so we move closer. We're apprehensive. Frozen with fear. We inch toward her, dreading the worst. And, just as we begin to feel the first waves of relief, a weight lifting off our hearts—she doesn't have any gunshot wounds, the thing hanging from her mouth is merely drool—the room is abruptly flooded with light. This flash announces the entrance of our most-forgotten True Creator, Moca. It would seem ten thirty AM is the best time to catch him in a state of wakefulness.

Maja jerks abruptly to life and, with a pained expression, attempts to lift her head. Moca must be ravenous, for he doesn't notice Maja at all as he walks past her on his way to the refrigerator. While the writer appears underwhelmed by the selection, he eventually retrieves a can of sardines, a jar of ajvar,[1] and half a loaf of bread. He grabs a knife from the drawer and, in cheerful naiveté, sets everything down on the table opposite Maja. He sits. The air crackles with a gluttonous charge as Moca prepares to break his fast. He opens the jar of ajvar, peers inside, sniffs it, and then uses the knife to scrape off the thin layer of mould which has formed on top. He happily spreads it on each slice, and then sandwiches the sardines between the slices. At last, the first bite reaches Moca's mouth, followed by moments of pure joy. Chewing and swallowing.

"Enjoy your meal," a female voice exhorts ironically from...somewhere. This unexpected intrusion startles Moca so much that he jumps up from his chair, spits a half-chewed bite onto the floor, and screams hysterically.

One by one, the True Creators rush down the stairs. First Voja, then Borojević, and finally Đorđe. The after effects of last night's altercation is plain on all three, but Đorđe, by all indications, seems to have gotten the worst of it. The right eye of the True Creator's elder statesman is purple and nearly swollen shut.

"Moco! Calm yourself! Moco, what's wrong?!" Voja grabs him by the shoulders and shakes him, but a still-terrified Moca continues to scream.

In time though, his screams soften to a whimper, and he seems to settle back into his body... Finally silent, Moca fixes to

---

1. Balkan red bell pepper and eggplant spread.

his peers with a deeply unsettled gaze. His fellow members of the Club of True Creators do their best to bring him up to speed, fairly competing to relate all of the exciting developments since he'd last been with them, consciously at least. With a flourish, Đorđe attempts to draw the story to a close on the whole company's behalf:

"And so, dearest Moco, as of yesterday, our Club is officially at war with all representatives of the liberal literary establishment!"

The man is an inexhaustible engine of pomposity, grandiose and significant words tumbling from his mouth in an unending stream. We wonder whether he was born into this world in the usual way, or was instead discovered gestating between the lines of *The Mountain Wreath*. After Đorđe's contribution, it's difficult for anyone else to add their thoughts. His puffed-up pronouncements and high-flown rhetoric cast a heavy silence once again, the room thick with deep emotion and elevated thoughts. The chests of the True Creators swell with pride, their collective gaze lost in distant glories of the future. Well, everyone except for Moca. His gaze rests firmly upon the glories of his recently-prepared sandwich.

"Personally, I would describe yesterday as more of a fratricidal war," Maja remarks from the side, the True Creators glaring daggers in reply.

"So, like, who is she, anyway?" Moca asks his colleagues, fully recovered and taking a long-delayed bite. "Excuse me, fellas, I'm just really hungry."

"You mean you *don't* know who she is?!" Voja smirks, in an effort to turn the tables on Maja's earlier claim of ignorance. He continues sarcastically, "That, Moco, is Miss Maja Trnavac, the High Commissar for Social Consciousness, a dedicated critic of Truth, and a missionary of empty European culture, aiming to destroy everything that's authentically ours. She fights against aestheticism, against *l'art pour l'art*. She is, in short, an enemy to our Club's most cherished values!"

"Ah. And her name is Marija...?"

"*Maja Trnavac!*"

"Ah," Moca repeats and then, losing interest, "Do you have any wine about, Vojo? It would go well with this fish."

All at once, everyone takes stock of Moca's breakfast. They exchange sidelong glances, and grimace in disgust. Voja goes to the pantry and produces some screw-top Riesling, which, having darkened with age, now looks more like a rosé.

"Excuse me for interrupting, gentlemen, but I really need the restroom," Maja says, calmly but urgently.

The True Creators scowl at first but, after a brief discussion and debate—which excludes the still-bingeing Moca—they resolve to grant her request. Voja approaches her from behind, cuts the tape binding her with his Swiss Army knife, and then guides her roughly to the outhouse. Maja stops abruptly short of the door.

"I really can't use that," she insists, following multiple attempts by Voja to push her inside.

"There's no other option. Either go in there or soil yourself."

"Really? *Really?*"

"Yes, 'really!' What's the hold-up, princess?"

"No, it's not like...*that*. I have a phobia of outhouses. When I was a girl, I watched a movie where a man fell through the hole and literally drowned in excrement."

"We should be so lucky!"

"But...actually, can't I just go in that cornfield?"

"No way."

"Please. I'll wet myself. Your chair will be ruined, and it'll stink like socially-conscious European piss..."

Torn, Voja looks left and right, and eventually relents with a grunt. But the negotiation isn't over: While Voja is adamant that Maja remain in his sight, she herself expresses an understandable reluctance to expose herself and pee in front of him. In a rare burst of common sense, Voja reluctantly accepts that there's no other feasible path available to him. Furious, he wishes he could slap her and push her back into the outhouse; instead, he begrudgingly turns his back and grumbles impotently.

He grumbles about her flimsy ideological agenda, about profit-motivated artists who refuse to leave their comfort zones, about European funds which are designed to homogenise national cultures, the intentional marginalisation of True Creators by a self-proclaimed cultural elite, arrogant dilettantes from the EU who dare to lecture others about human rights, media freedoms, dialogue, and other phantoms and fantasies of the twenty-first century. Voja continues in this vein for some time, and, and, and—and then he stops. Our protagonist has been facing away from his captive for some time now. He bends his head and takes as brief and unvoyeuristic a peek as he can muster...

"EMERGENCYYY!" Voja screams at the top of his lungs into endless, empty rows of corn.

18

In a spacious, grey office, we are reunited with our favourite BIA agents. The hulking Milovan sits in a mustard-coloured leather armchair, restlessly twirling his mobile phone. In his gigantic hand, it looks no bigger than a Zippo lighter. His hairy, cruel, tennis-playing superior stands at the window with a stormy expression, hands in pockets. His lips are pressed so tightly that he might never speak again, a defiant boy in a dentist's chair.

An oppressive silence fills the room, occasionally pierced by the sounds of heavy traffic from Novi Sad's Liberation Boulevard. And Milovan, for all his size, is hardly dim-witted. He knows full well what's coming his way and, under the circumstances, prefers to suffer his commanding agent's rage sooner rather than later. In an attempt to subtly provoke the older agent into at least the opening phases of reprimand, Milovan ventures a plausibly innocent: "Well, this has been a pretty shitty day."

The older agent takes a deep breath, squints, and begins to stroke his eyebrow with a single finger, unmistakably signalling that his distilled anger has yet to crest. Things have turned unmistakably grimmer for Milovan than they were moments ago. "Boss...," he starts.

He should've stayed silent. There's no going back now. Some of our number advocate an immediate retreat—"We'll be collateral damage!" "Let's see what Milonja and Nataša are up to!"—while others can't tear their eyes away from the impending explosion. The latter group leans in as they watch the colossal man in the chair collapse timidly into himself, his superior suddenly a furious predator looming over him. Milovan mumbles some perfunctory last-ditch excuses under his breath; we get the impression that he's attempting to shift the blame onto their unit in Belgrade.

"You better listen up, you incompetent meathead!" The elder agent's long-awaited tirade begins at last. "And, honestly, you needn't explain a thing! Why defend yourself, Gvozdenović? I admire you! Truly, I do! Yes! I admire the skill with which you and your men have completely lost track of a pair of nobodies, with no special skills."

"But..."

"Not just yet, Milovan, don't you dare, because the best has yet to come: a Renault 4! For fuck's sake, you managed to lose an old man and a worn-out woman in a bright red Renault 4! Meatheads! Imbeciles! You, you...!"

"But, boss, Trajković didn't..."

"And what the hell does Trajković have to do with anything?!"

"I just mean..."

"Nope, don't even! The gumption, to manage even a single word—how do you do it? If I were in your shoes, I'd have shrunk to a speck of dust and floated down the Danube! But still, *you* have the nerve to make excuses. The betrayal! Oh, Milovan... How could you do this to me?"

"Banjac was..."

Thwack! Milovan's skull resonates like a drum, but both men act as if nothing has happened. Honestly, we're hardly sure ourselves now—everything happened so fast.

Although the boss pulls his arm back to strike again, he checks himself at the last moment and takes a breath. The weary older agent shoves his hands back into his pockets, walks over to the window, and says:

"We screwed up."

"But we'll find them, it's just a matter of time. I've brought in five more guys."

"Even if you brought in fifty, Gvozdenović, there's no chance. We'll only find them at this point when they choose to show up, and by then it'll be too late. Half of Serbia will be hailing them as heroes. I can see it already."

"What? Haven't you seen our smear campaign? *Heroes?* How?"

"I don't know how...but I know. We definitely screwed up."

Had there been a record playing in the background, at this moment, the needle would surely have reached its end, skipping and producing a repetitive, grating sound. But in the nondescript office, there's nothing. The only sound is the muffled, impatient revving of a sports car outside at the intersection. "Milovan, did you call the hospital to check on Pešut?"

"I did. Nothing new."

"Nothing at all? He still doesn't remember...*anything?*"

"Not a thing."

For the next minute or two, perhaps even a whole five, literally nothing noteworthy happens. Eyes are rubbed. Yawns proliferate. So soon after the excitement of violence, the very real possibility of dozing off in the BIA office becomes the greater threat... But then, a new face suddenly enters the room.

Or rather, the face is new to us, but old to the world—lined and desperate. The newcomer looks from Milovan to the senior agent, who both return his gaze in expectation. But the man seems hesitant, even nervous.

"Come on, chief, speak up already! What's bothering the beat cops in Novi Sad today?" the older security agent asks dismissively.

"We've brought in an old man who claims he saw Milonja and Nataša entering the apartment across from his today around noon. He says they're still inside," the newcomer finally says, then looks expectantly between the agents, waiting for some question or at least acknowledgement. But the security agents just exchange glances and say nothing.

Well, at first, they say nothing. Then, after a pause: "Really? And how does he know they're still in there? Is some old lady peeping through a spyhole and reporting back?" the senior agent scoffs, and Milovan soon joins in with a chuckle. "Well, I guess," replies the bewildered newcomer, who is grinning nervously himself, having no better response. "Do you want me to bring him up?"

"God, no! Are you mad? We get one of these Čvorović types every day![1] It's so annoying."

"Sorry, I didn't intend to... I didn't mean... I mean, we probably could have handled this without you, but given the sensitivity of the whole situation, I wanted to make sure that..."

"All right, all right, chief. We get it. Gvozdenović, grab one of your guys, and let's take this geezer home to debrief."

"But there's no chance they're in Novi Sad, we..."

"I know, Milovan, I know, but this is the only way to get the city police off our backs. Trust me. Let's go."

The BIA agents head for the door but, just as they cross the threshold, the cop chances:

"Excuse me, ah, what should I do? Should I follow you?"

"No. Absolutely not. Chief, you stay here, hold down the fort. And maybe make a sandwich or two; we'll be hungry when we return."

The mean-spirited laughter of the older security agent and his young associate echoes down the hall, while, right before our eyes, the bewildered Chief of the Novi Sad Police Department withers into a pitiful, shrunken husk, devoid of any unique identifying features. Except, maybe, a stench.

---

1. A reference to 1984's Balkanski špijun ("Balkan Spy"), a film about a busybody named Ilija Čvorović who becomes convinced that his tenant is a spy and threat to the socialist system.

19

OUR CONFUSION AT THE new scene before us is profound. In the middle of a cornfield, Vojislav Počuča hovers, an overinflated parade balloon. Our protagonist frantically surveys the field, while almost his entire upper half hovers above the high, golden stalks.

Bowler hat screwed tightly on his head, Voja squints from behind thick glasses in an attempt to deepen his field of vision and locate the fleeing Maja among the cornstalks. The scene is sufficiently surreal that several of us fidget and rub our eyes, mouths agape. A few even grumble, suspicious that the story of the Club of True Creators has taken an unwelcome turn to magical realism. However, tensions calm when we approach close enough to divine the mechanism behind Voja's levitation. His fellow True Creators are, in fact, simply holding him aloft, Borojević and Đorđe anchoring one of Voja's legs each.

"My God, for a moment I thought the man's ego had inflated enough to blow him up," one of us titters, "Imagine if people's heights were actually, in fact, determined by their egos. That would be a charming fancy, would it not?"

Our group takes a moment to consider the girl's proposal and immediately realises that, quite the contrary, it wouldn't be charming at all. The humble and polite would dangle helplessly like chewed gum from the shoes of titans, while the latter admire their reflections in the windows of skyscrapers.

"Do you see her anywhere, Vojo?" Đorđe manages to gasp, from under his colleague's considerable weight.

"She's gone," answers Voja. "As if she vanished into thin air."

"Bring him down," Borojević says and, together with Đorđe, they release our protagonist to the mercy of gravity and the rich Fruška Gora soil.

At first, the dismount looks good. Actually, better than good: impressive even.

Voja's steel-toed cowboy boots dig into the loose soil, as if he had just dismounted from a horse, a quick-footed sheriff from the American Old West. But then the poor writer buckles on his left leg and, through some intermediary phases of collapse, ultimately finds his face flat on the ground. He stretches his body out in the furrow, and his bowler rolls off his head. The hat wheels away lazily for a couple of metres before twirling and coming to rest. None of the True Creators initially grasps what has happened, least of all Voja himself.

Stunned, he lies prone for some time before his colleagues from the Club rush in to help. They lift him cautiously, and Đorđe, concern evident in his voice, asks if he's doing OK. Voja doesn't speak, staring hazily through extravagantly askew glasses. Borojević offers Voja a swig of rakija from his flask, but he waves it away, and attempts to stand. The attempt is a wobbly one however, his centre of gravity seeming to have shifted somehow outside his body. Voja shuffles to his hat, picks it up, dusts it off, screws it back on his head, and sets off with great purpose...and no evident destination.

The other Creators exchange bewildered glances and watch frozen as Voja staggers through the corn, a drunk tumbling out from last call. They follow him haltingly, calling out to him in turns, and hoping that he will stop. But no, their colleague is a man on a mission. Although they lose sight of Voja, Đorđe and Borojević follow the trail of flattened stalks, praying each second for an end to this seemingly infinite expanse of corn.

After a few minutes of tracking Voja, they finally emerge from the field...and find themselves immediately face to face with a not-especially-friendly dog, baring its teeth and growling deeply. Very deeply in fact, because apart from being not-especially-friendly, the dog is also not-especially-small. Truly, life is full of surprises. From corn to grapes, produce has been unkind to our True Creators; now most especially concerned with their own safety, Đorđe's colleagues allow his situation to recede in urgency. Both men freeze.

We've seen this scene plenty of times in Hollywood movies: guard dogs, usually Dobermans or Rottweilers, standing face to face with intruders, then chasing them in a fury only to be outpaced by the heroes. But this dog is touchably, smellably, murderously close, and we feel our own confidence begin to drain along with that of the True Creators.

Borojević whispers to Đorđe, his eyes never leaving the dog's bared, slobbery fangs: "Đorđe, what should we do? Do you have your gun?"

Borojević earns a deep growl by way of reply, but not from Đorđe. After a moment, Borojević tries again, just as softly and cautiously, "Should we...?"

Before he can finish the question, Đorđe clutches suddenly at his chest and falls haltingly to the ground in multiple, dramatic stages. He ends up flat on the ground, in a community theatre facsimile of death. A tense, baffled silence follows. Both Borojević and the dog stare at Đorđe in open confusion.

Lying rigidly on the Fruška Gora soil in his formal attire, bereft of any human dignity, Đorđe is fooling no one—not us, not Borojević, and not the dog. Especially not the dog. With its ears drooping and gaze lowered, the dog approaches Đorđe with a terrifying deliberateness, but is halted midway by a thin cord tying it to a nearby tree. While the dog doesn't seem too surprised by this, Borojević certainly is. He stares at the cord, which might as well have appeared in the grass by divine intervention, and allows a wave of relief and joy to wash over him before addressing the deceased:

"Đorđe, get up."

The gentlemanly author remains motionless, betraying no signs of life. He won't be fooled so easily.

"The dog is tied up, Đorđe. You can get up," Borojević urges him with a gentle shake.

It's unlikely Đorđe could open both eyes if he wanted to, but he now opens one of them to peer up at Borojević and assess the situation. Hesitantly and taking no risks with his safety, he ultimately heeds his colleague's advice and rises to his feet. The éminence grise of the True Creators moves with such stately grace, every motion filled with confidence and dignity, that we quickly forget the earlier foolishness. The only reminder of that unfortunate interlude is the soil on his suit, which he brushes off with vigorous hand movements, as if offended by this inexplicable contamination. For reasons known only to it, the dog is similarly offended by Đorđe's hand movements and begins to snarl and bark with renewed vigour.

"Đorđe, did you bring the gun?" Borojević asks.

"No, I left it back at the cottage. I'd barely woken up when the other one shouted 'Emergency!'" Đorđe replies.

"Ah well," says Borojević. "Fuck it. Should we just head back then? I'm starving."

"Yeah, let's get going, just let me..." Đorđe trails off, fixes his gaze on the dog, and hurls an ear of corn at it, which naturally infuriates the creature. Borojević finds this wildly entertaining and eagerly grabs an ear of his own to throw. But Đorđe takes it a step further and begins to thrash the dog with the full length of the stalk itself, smacking the beast enough to enrage if not to maim. The dog growls, gasps, whimpers, barks—the whole spectrum of canine discontent—as the True Creators assault it with corn.

Several minutes of this torment fail to diminish the dog's resolve to tear them limb from limb. Exhausted, the Creators finally give up and turn back to Voja's cottage. After about twenty yards, Borojević breaks off a valedictory ear of corn, lobs it full-force at the dog, and scores a bullseye, which delights them both.

The delight, however, is short lived. In a final burst of retaliatory fury, the dog yanks on its tether with sufficient force to snap it clean in two. The animal hesitates for a moment in surprise, just long enough for the creators to do the same and then bolt, top speed, in opposite directions.

In the sudden chaotic confusion, it's hard to know where to look. We start following one, then the other, then back to the first...and eventually find ourselves stuck in the middle of the field, paralyzed by indecision. Ultimately, we conclude with a brave face that this is probably for the best—no reason to inflict such Tarantino-esque carnage on the more sensitive members of our group.

However, at the end of this dramatic and somewhat distressing chapter—an interlude which might deservedly prompt the interest of animal rights activists—a critical question emerges: Had Đorđe Smolović actually died, would he have evoked more or less sympathy from us than he did by merely pretending?

20

SHARING NATAŠA AND MILONJA'S company isn't particularly easy. The two of them sit silently in the monastery courtyard, but this isn't the kind of silence one might encounter in the reading room of the Matica Srpska[1] or in the depths of the Adriatic Sea. No. This silence is charged with unspoken concerns, worries, and a whole constellation of swirling emotions. Each of us has, at some point in our lives, found ourselves in a similar situation—struck mute by the paralysis of cognitive function, triggered by the rush of adrenaline and the frenzied beating of one's heart.

From an outsider's perspective, the pair's inability to start a conversation, despite an evident desire to do so, is almost touching. Time passes, nothing happens. Nataša lights a second cigarette, moments after stubbing out her first. Milonja starts feeling cold, and gets up to walk around and stave off the chill of nerves and cold alike. With each step he takes, the tension seems

---

1. The "Serbian Matica." Maticas are national foundations which date to the era of foreign domination in the Balkans. The reference here is to the library's silence.

to ratchet up a notch, and the atmosphere grows even more uncomfortable. We wonder how this bubble of pent-up tension might ever have resolved, had Nataša not suddenly blurted out:

"For heaven's sake, Šoškić! I really don't need your pacing right now!"

Milonja, taken aback, stops abruptly. Had he attempted words in that moment, he would have surely stammered. Although Nataša regards him—frozen as he is in awkwardness—with transparent affection and empathy, she continues sternly:

"Why don't you try another call, Milonja? Your guy *must* have looked into it by now."

"No, Nataša! You've made me call him five times now. I'm not doing it a sixth. The doctor told me the third time that there was no need to pester him, and that he'd call as soon as he had any information."

"I know, I know he said that. But what if he forgot though??"

"Forget? He will one hundred percent remember me, Nataša. I called him five times in less than three hours. *Five times!*"

"Okay, you called. Yes, you did..."

Through the peaks and (mostly) troughs of his adult life, Milonja had felt particularly blessed by good fortune. When he suddenly felt the vibration of his mobile phone in his pocket, however, he looked skyward in a silent prayer of gratitude, the luckiest man alive.

The conversation with the doctor was brief, five minutes at most, but Nataša watched Milonja intently every second, trying to make at least some educated guesses. This proved nearly impossible, however, since her companion's replies were almost exclusively limited to *I see*'s and *Aha*'s. Milonja threw in a couple *Mm-hmm*'s towards the end and then, in a sesquipedalian spasm: "Thank you so very much, Doctor!"

"Well?"

"Pešut is fine."

"Really?!" Nataša fairly beamed, but only for a second. "Wait, what do you mean, 'fine'?"

"Just that. The doctor said they expect to send him home tomorrow."

"Send him *home?* That makes zero sense. He was literally run all the way over by a car."

Milonja switches to body language, conveying to Nataša through gestures and facial expressions that he stands fully behind what he's said, that there's no reason to doubt, that the doctor is trustworthy and wouldn't lie to him.

At first, Nataša scrutinises Milonja with confusion, furrowing her brow and trying to make sense of things. Then, slowly at first and then all of a sudden, she permits a wave of happiness to wash over her. It begins in her stomach, spreads first to her chest, then to her throat, her cheeks, and settles finally on her lips. She notices she can no longer feel her own hands, and then realises that this is because they have enveloped a stunned police inspector in a joyful hug. The poor man stands there stiff as a board, his eyes darting around in disbelief, searching in vain for some action, any action to take.

Instead of returning the embrace and surrendering to the wave of affection, Milonja reluctantly murmurs, "He has amnesia."

Nataša pulls back slightly, processing his words. "He what?"

"The doctor said Pešut can't remember anything. He has amnesia."

"You mean he doesn't remember the accident? That he doesn't know how he ended up in the hospital?"

"Well, yes. But, from what I understood, he doesn't know who he is or where he's from. Nothing at all. Complete and total memory loss."

As the implications of an amnesiac war criminal begin to wash over Nataša, so does a wave of vertigo. Just in time, Milonja reaches out to support her.

"This is too much, Milonja… I cannot fucking believe it! Why would it…why would he…? How bloody…ironic."

"Come on now, you make it sound like you wish he had died instead!"

"At this point, I'm not sure. Maybe it would've been better. The whole point was to show him that some crimes can never be forgotten, that the people remember…" Her voice begins to tremble. "And now I've done the exact opposite. Pešut himself won't know what he's done. It's just not fair!"

Tears stream unselfconsciously down Nataša's face. She blames herself for bringing a criminal inner peace, the uncomplicated purity of a newborn. She curses herself as an amateur, an imbecile, a madwoman, and a loser. She wishes she were dead. Through all of this, Milonja does his best to console her; she could not, of course, have foreseen this outcome. But she remains inconsolable.

By this point, it is abundantly clear that Milonja regrets mentioning Pešut's amnesia at all. He wishes that he could turn the clock back to that embrace, remaining silent the second time around...

"Nataša, you're not a fool at all! I think...I think you're wonderful!" he blurts, surprising them both. She blushes. Their eyes meet. The moment hangs heavily in the air. A couple of us try briefly to compare the scene with this romcom or that one...but for most of us, it doesn't matter. Love itself, the genuine article, is unfolding right in front of us. Love in its purest form, in the shared gaze, in the electricity crackling in the space between, in memories of the past, in dreams of the future, in the goosebumps prickling their skin, in the now, in their fingers, in...the courtyard of a monastery. Hollywood clichés dictate that such moments should culminate in a passionate kiss. But alas, Abbot Stefan, monastically unaware of such clichés, suddenly appears at a distance, shouting at full volume:

"What's the matter, Nataša? Why are you crying? Did he tell you one of his jokes or something?" As the pair's reaction is, to put it mildly, underwhelmed, the priest does pick up a slightly awkward vibe. However, hoping for a better reception on the second attempt, he shrugs off the feeling and animatedly relays the various rumours swirling around them on Serbian gossip sites. The priest underlines his shock at the sites' content by paraphrasing these articles in some detail—although in deference to his station, Abbot Stefan elects to censor one particularly untoward headline before quoting it. Ultimately, the abbot advises them to stay out of Serbia for the foreseeable future. Further silence meets this dramatic conclusion.

Growing mildly concerned by his guests' catatonia, the priest glances first at Nataša, then at Milonja, and then back to Nataša. He waves his hand in front of their eyes.

"Hello? Can you hear me? I suggest we call my editor friend Lakobrija and get this in his paper, the sooner the better."

"...I'm not sure that makes sense," Milonja replies at last.

"How do you mean? Of course, it makes sense. It's the truth!"

"Sure, my brother. But people get discredited all the time precisely *because* they approached journalists before the authorities."

"Mile, old friend, I understand you're tired and stressed, but what are you talking about? Please look at this rationally. The two of you are already being smeared as foreign agents. You *will* be accused of espionage. You get that, right?"

Milonja looks away in silence. Nataša follows suit.

"Please, please listen to me," the monk pleads, pressing his hands together and holding them close to Milonja's face.

Milonja regards his friend and offers a small but honest smile while weighing his reply. He glances towards Nataša, perhaps for some support, but she seems lost in a world entirely of her own, staring blankly while absentmindedly stroking one of her canine companions.

We can't deny that Stefan is, for a monastic priest, dynamic, proactive, and—yes—impatient. Sensing Milonja's hesitation, the abbot fills the silence with further arguments to stay put, trying to convince them that—

"All right, all right, Stevo, you win. We'll call your journalist friend," Milonja reluctantly concedes, before adding: "but he'll need to guarantee not to publish until we give the green light."

"*That's* what I like to hear, Mile! I'm sure he'll agree. You know it makes sense."

"Well, actually..." Milonja paused for a moment. "I'm not sure if Nataša agrees. What do you think?" Nataša stares hazily for a moment before apologising:

"I'm really sorry, gentlemen. I'm just...preoccupied I guess..." She stands abruptly, walks off, and then immediately returns. Muttering something under her breath, she wavers for a moment...and then confidently sets off in the complete opposite direction. She returns and repeats the complete process again, halting, turning, and retracing her steps at full speed.

Nataša at last comes to rest in front of Milonja, who watches her with a perplexed but deep affection. With a teary-eyed smile, she hesitantly extends her hands, first one, then the other. He flushes a deep red, his heart skipping a beat because he sees that...

B i b b i d i - b o b b i d i - b o o! And the scene is transformed into a Disney fairytale—their mutual tenderness fills us with such sweetness and light that it's almost like falling in love ourselves. If, due to the spell of an old voodoo sorcerer, Milonja had been enchanted and presented to Nataša as a frog, there's no doubt that this is the moment at which he would turn into a dashing and handsome prince.

Of course, we're all grownups: real life isn't a fairytale and miracles don't happen. But still. It doesn't stop Father Stefan from making the sign of the cross and looking to the heavens when the bell tower chimes. *A blessing from the divine*, he thinks. And it doesn't stop us from thinking the same.

Blessing it may have been but, when the priest's eyes return from the heavens to his watch, he realises that evening service started five minutes ago, and he's the one leading it. The abbot scrambles off to the church and we... well, we might have remained in the courtyard for hours enchanted by the scene before us, if only Nataša's dogs hadn't growled and chased us away.

21

"TO BE CLEAR, THE suspects are in that apartment? Right now?" Milovan Gvozdenović asks the elderly couple, indicating the door across the hall.

The old couple exchange a bespectacled look, turn back, and with a simultaneous nod, confirm a total absence of doubt.

"And you are absolutely certain?" asks the younger BIA agent who has joined Milovan on this interview. Even though the Grandpa and Grandma reaffirm their certainty, their confidence is visibly less pronounced. The agents exchange wary glances.

They show the couple photographs of the fugitives once more, and insist that they take a closer look this time before answering. In an effort to improve their concentration, Grandpa removes his hat and scratches his head, while Grandma takes the photos gingerly between her hands and scrutinises them intently. First up close, then from a distance, turning them left and then right, and finally handing them to her husband.

He takes his turn, holds his temples, and studies the photographs closely, deep in thought. Before returning the images to the security agents, he whispers something to his wife. She takes the photos once more, removes her husband's glasses and places them in front of her own smaller ones, in an attempt to supercharge her visual acuity. Her lip-smacking and teeth grinding suggest the intensity of her struggle.

The agents have grown impatient in the meantime, their increasing restlessness solicitous of a conclusion. The old woman remains undeterred by their subtle coughs and tuts of impatience, however.

Then, all of a sudden, the front door of the apartment in question swings open, and two individuals emerge who could not be more dissimilar from those in the photos: a young Korean couple in their twenties, most likely graduate students at the university. They greet the security agents and elderly couple alike in passable Serbian and, without skipping a beat, Grandma hands the photos back to the agents, and declares proudly:

"We're certain it's them!"

22

IF WE WERE TO sum up the atmosphere at Voja's cottage on Fruška Gora with a single word, "gloomy" would rank highly among our candidates. Nothing in the room, not a single element, escapes that description. Even the scant daylight escaping through the window shutters only underscores just how dusty the room is.

Moca drowsily lounges on a couch draped in a stained, brown blanket; Borojević nibbles on a corn cob while a thin column of smoke drifts lazily from his ashtray; and Voja sits on the third stair step, fully dressed in his coat and bowler, playing chess on his phone. We can't help but wonder: are these the same men who, whooping in comradeship and brotherhood, only yesterday burst forth from the True Creators' clubhouse ready for battle?

Yes, they are.

But, since then, the Club has faced countless challenges to their valour. The team has lost its direction. Their morale has bottomed out. Voja, after being checkmated for a fifth time in a row by an inanimate object, despondently thinks that his life has become an endless stream of shit. He nearly throws his phone against the wall, but checks himself at the last moment and places it next to him on the step. Agitated and bored—a perilous combination.

Voja casts a sidelong gaze at Borojević for over a minute before alighting on the perfect catalyst for a quarrel. Borojević is prepared for the unprovoked assault, however, and accusations fly back and forth, too quickly to follow. To be sure, we hear about the recent business with Maja and the dog, but also an incident at a poetry festival in Zrenjanin that both had apparently attended in 1989. In Voja's telling, a jealous Borojević persuaded the festival's organiser, an old university friend, to switch the lineup at the last minute. This event proves to be the final straw, and the two men's neck veins bulge as their bickering reaches a fever pitch. Moca, groggy with sleep and rakija, is forced reluctantly to his senses. At any moment they might come to blows. The feuding colleagues shove each other, threatening new vengeance with each new affront. Abruptly however, Borojević shifts tactics, his voice dropping to a gentle but icy whisper.

"You know, though? I do understand that it's tough when a peer consistently outshines you. It's not the best time for you, I know, but you'll find out soon enough: I've got two major successes coming down the line. Let us draw this pointless argument to a close, my dear friend. An argument," Borojević adds kindly, "in which I would thoroughly have crushed you."

Voja plays along, responding with a cynical smile, "You're too thoughtful, Boro. But please, don't trouble yourself: You couldn't upset me by bragging about fifty-two major successes. Success is relative, after all. And all your 'successes'"—he air quotes—"won't change the fact that your books are painfully boring, repetitive, and flat-out stupid. If not for Đorđe, you'd never have been accepted here among us, the True Creators."

"Oh really? Well, screw you and your Club! I'm out."

"What?! You can't just..."

"I don't give a damn! Moca, are you coming or staying?"

"Well...," Moca considers.

"You're staying," Voja answers for him, "and so is Boro. He's an asshole, but he's not going to strand us on Fruška Gora without a car."

But it seems that Borojević really has reached that level of asshole, for he waves his hand dismissively and strolls for the exit. In that instant, however, Đorđe bursts opportunely through the cottage doors into the living room. Or, more accurately, what remains of him bursts into the living room.

"Đorđe!" The True Creators share the same stunned expression. If we hadn't been acquainted with Đorđe already, we'd have concluded that he was a circus announcer mauled by a lion with nothing left to lose. His right trouser leg is shredded. The left one is torn up to the knee, revealing a patchwork of bloody scratches. Wild-eyed, dust-covered as a miner when the whistle blows, and a left hand swollen to twice its natural size... he could fairly hear his late mother chiding, "Dear heart, how many times have I told you to change out of your good clothes before running out in the field? The state of you!"

Đorđe doesn't even make it as far as the chair. He stumbles at the threshold and crashes to the floor. After recovering from their collective shock, his Club colleagues rush to the aid of their most distinguished colleague. Together, they lift him up and...

"Where should we put him?" Borojević wonders aloud, Đorđe hovering heavily between the two colleagues. Voja glances around and directs, "Bring him over to the couch. Moca, get up!"

Moca groans and grunts, but finally manages to tear himself from the couch's invisible but powerful magnetic pull. Holding his left arm and muffling his cries, his colleagues lower Đorđe gently onto the seat.

"I was looking for you, Đorđe, but then—" Borojević begins, before Voja cuts in:

"We were all looking for you, Smolović! Where were you? It was like you vanished off the face of the earth."

While an anxious fear in Smolović's eyes conveys an eagerness to speak, nothing but a guttural sound escapes his deadlocked jaw. There is no doubt that this is a man experiencing clinical shock and in need of urgent medical attention. The True Creators are so disturbed by this turn of events, however, that all they can muster is a collective impotent stare in Đorđe's general direction.

"How... are you doing, Đorđe?" Moca finally ventures from the back, breaking the uncomfortable silence. The others' heads turn slowly to him, hoping that they have misheard. Đorđe's eyes bulge, his hiss hardly registering as human speech. We get the gist though: *Do you mock me?!*

We have, all of us, asked stupid questions in our lives and suffered the consequences, but Moca is sufficiently well-tippled that most would give him a pass. He returns his colleagues' anxious stares with a blissfully innocent blankness. Đorđe starts to gurgle. The others lean in. They guess wildly at his charades and, with each failed attempt, Đorđe's frustration grows. Had he not possessed a functional right hand, with which to mime drinking from a glass, he might have died of thirst.

Voja leaps up to pour water from a bottle he finds in the fridge, tending to his fallen comrade like the Maiden nursing Pavle Orlović on Blackbird's Field.[1] The first drops have scarcely touched Đorđe's throat, when he lets out a painful cry. All the True Creators take a step back, including Đorđe, who has leapt to his feet, roaring:

"I SAID WATER!"

While Đorđe's insides continue to roil, Voja scrambles for the bottle, and then recoils at the scent of moonshine distilled by his neighbour—five years ago? Before he passed away, that much is certain. He dives for the pack of water bottles they'd left by the entrance, doing his best to beat Borojević to the punch. Voja is

---

1. The Maiden of the Blackbird's Field, is a classic Serbian epic poem. Its protagonist is a beautiful young woman, the "Kosovo Maiden," who searches a battlefield for her beloved and tends to fallen soldiers (like Orlović) along the way. In the end, her beloved is already dead. The name Kosovo means "the blackbird's" in Serbian, and refers to the titular field.

a touch slower, but still manages to get a firm grasp. Now, the two squabble like schoolboys:

"Let go, Vojo, I got it first!"

"Don't even start! It's my water—I bought it!"

"It's all of our water! You bought it with Club funds. Just let go already! Can't you see—?"

"You let go, Boro!"

"I won't! You first!"

"Not on my life! You drop it!"

"Let it go!"

"Never! I was first..."

Suddenly, an awareness of the argument's pettiness descends on both squabbling writers...especially since Moca has, in the meantime, located a different water bottle from which Đorđe is greedily glugging. Now, the creators wait for Đorđe to say or do something. He says nothing. He does less. The Creators hope that this is simply him creating intentional dramatic tension, as is his wont in better times. But the fear grows that their most gentlemanly colleague has simply lost the power of speech. That this succession of psychological traumas has left him incapacitated. So, now what?

Suddenly, Đorđe lifts his head, and they are able to look directly into his unfocused eyes, each wandering its own path while a foolish grin spreads across his face. It looks as if some kind-hearted thief has burgled his brain, sparing him of all life's concerns. He sways like a drunkard. Voja remarks that vodka can in fact be quite the elixir, and recounts how his neighbour's mother-in-law swears by three shots a day for asthma. Moca joins in with an exhaustive treatise on vodka—its history, manner of production, varietals, subvarietals, and various medicinal properties. Somewhere amidst their speechifying, Đorđe staggers backward and crumples again to the floor, returning the True Creators to a state of panic.

"Đorđe!"

"Check if he's breathing! What do we do?!"

"Đorđe!"

"He's breathing."

"Give him CPR."

"I *just said* that he's breathing!"

"Đorđe, can you hear me?"

"Damn it, are you out of your mind?!"

"Why?"

"Why are you dousing him? You want him to drown?!" Filthy, ragged, bitten, and scratched, with a black eye and swollen left hand, pale as chalk and now thoroughly soaked from a water bottle, Đorđe finds himself on a perilous path. On one side awaits the warmth of friendship's embrace, and on the other lurks the menacing abyss of unconsciousness.

After a brief deliberation, the True Creators decide it's best not to leave things to chance. They bundle their wounded friend into Borojević's car and tear off to the Provincial Hospital. With the power of teamwork, the Club manages an impressive speed. Just as Voja steps outside and pulls out his keys to lock the door, he hears the distant ring of a mobile phone from inside the cottage. Following the sound, he reaches an old dresser, grabs Maja's purse with the phone inside, and turns quickly on his heel back out of the house. A few claustrophobes among us immediately start to sweat and lament our return to the overcrowded and tiny vehicle. But we can put these worries to rest—the omnipotence of literature allows us to pause this scene and escape to a more spacious one in the next chapter.

23

HERE WE ARE AGAIN in Banjska. It's a pleasant evening, the sky starry and clear, with the mildest of nips in the air. Quiet, certainly, but then we are after all in a monastery courtyard. All in all, the scene seems tailor-made for a couple in love, arms intertwined and gazing up at the constellations. It warms our hearts to see the two lovebirds treating each other with such tenderness, all the more so when they aren't in the fullest springtime of their youth. Nataša raises her finger to trace patterns in the sky, and says something to Milonja which we can't quite hear from here. Let's get a bit closer.

"...and that's Pegasus, and just over there is Andromeda! A whole galaxy unto itself. In a few billion years, the Andromeda galaxy will collide with our own Milky Way"

"Oh no! And what should we do, how shall we escape?" Milonja teases, clearly delighted at the playful smile that he's drawn from Nataša's lips.

"There's nothing at all to be done! No escape."

But the sentiment is actually a bit unsettling, and reminds them of their current real-life mess. *No escape*, echoes in their minds. Milonja clears his throat, offers a wry smile, and, desperate to break the gloom, asks:

"So...what's your zodiac sign?"

Nataša looks at him nonplussed. She might have kept a straight face if his own weren't so serious, but can't quite manage it...

"I want you to guess."

Milonja sizes her up, scratches his chin. He takes his time, apparently plugging each facet of her personality individually into an astrological equation. After double checking his work, he responds:

"Virgo."

"Shut *up!*" Nataša seems thrilled. "How did you guess? You peeked at my ID when I opened my wallet, admit it!"

"Of course not, Nataša, why would you think that? I would never..." He places his right hand over his heart, projecting utmost sincerity.

"Well how, then? I have to know!"

"Honestly...I don't know," Milonja laughs. "My ex-wife was into astrology. She drafted these huge birth charts and made horoscopes for people. I probably picked up a thing or two along the way."

"Really?! That's so cool. And this ex, she's really just one of four?" Although Nataša seems nothing but curious and amused, Milonja doesn't share her enthusiasm for the topic. He responds with a subdued nod. "Well, kudos to her! Too bad she couldn't read the stars for herself and ended up with a dead-end playboy," Nataša teases, winking and tousling Milonja's hair. He blushes, and waves her off, *Oh yeah, such a charmer.*

"So, are you really a Virgo?" he asks. Nataša shugs and confesses:

"Aquarius."

"Aquarius?"

"Yep."

"I don't believe it. You must have Virgo as your rising sign."

"Oh, almost certainly," she agrees.

They both laugh and, caught up in the beauty of the moment, they fold into each other and kiss like uni students on a field trip... Well then! With the moment taking a turn for the intimate, some of us begin to wonder if we should take a step back. A bystander might think we're peeping toms or, worse, voyeurs who target lovers of a certain age. We begin to tiptoe backwards, quietly as we can...

"What about you?" Milonja's voice pierces the silence and freezes us in place.

Nataša looks blankly, a large neon question mark flickering above her head.

"I mean to say, ah, have you ever been married?"

"Oh, that! No, I haven't."

"Not even once?"

"Not even once. There was a close call twenty, wow, seven years ago, but it didn't happen."

"Why not?"

"Why not?"

"Yeah."

"He passed away."

"Oh man. Seriously?"

"Seriously."

Both fall into contemplation and, in their own ways, each tries to grapple with outrageous fortune's slings and arrows. Gazing again at the stars, they sift their memories, wondering if things could have turned out differently, whether destiny can ever be truly resisted, or if we are instead doomed to be eternally buffeted by the whims of fate. Is it possible that nothing is really up to us, in the end? Along their brief internal journeys of the soul, where old wounds reopen to pour out the heartache of youth, and near-forgotten joys are reawakened, the couple stumbles upon a profound thought from Epictetus: "Hope not that events will turn out the way you want, but welcome events in whichever way they happen: This is the path to peace."

Amidst the wisdom of ancients, chance, destiny, memory, and the Andromeda galaxy hurtling in their direction, Nataša and Milonja's eyes meet once more, here, in the courtyard of the Banjska Monastery in Kosovo. They remain silent for a while, sitting with the comfortable heaviness of the moment, before embracing again. Nataša whispers, scarcely louder than a thought:

"I wonder what will become of us?"

We wonder the same but, since Milonja remains silent, accept that the answer must be found elsewhere.

24

"DAMN THEM ALL TO hell! Did you hear me, Milovan?! I'm going to fucking *tear them apart!*" the senior BIA agent roars at the top of his lungs as he rummages through some drawers. Socks, underwear, shirts, and T-shirts fly backwards over his head in an arc. "Did you get *anything* from Milonja's colleagues? Anything at all, even a morsel?"

"Nothing at all, boss. For now. We have a ton of calls from citizens, though, from Surdulica and Temerin to Sombor and Zlatibor."

"For fuck's sake. Have they all seen them?"

"Every single one of them. Supposedly."

The elder security guard lets out a tortured groan. "But his colleagues on the force, though! They must know something, for God's sake!"

"Nothing. Just that he's normal, boring, keeps to himself. One of them gave us the name of a mutual acquaintance." Milovan scrolls briefly through his phone and reads, "'Nebojša Kešelj, Associate Professor at the Faculty of Technology.' We checked his apartment and cottage. Nothing."

"What do you mean 'nothing,' Milovan? How could there be nothing at all at the friend's place!?"

"I mean to say, the friend wasn't there anymore. Subtenant says that he moved with his family to Trondheim about six months ago. In Norway."

"Ooh, Norway, huh?" the older agent snaps. "You think I don't know where Trondheim is, so you need to inform me?"

"No no, I..."

"Whatever. Keep looking; we're not leaving until we find something usable. A to-do list, some photos..."

"His computer is password-protected; Lalović is bringing it to the IT guys."

Teasing apart the context clues, we come to realise that this is a raid on Milonja's apartment by the Serbian security-information agency. Some universal if secret police procedure appears to be at work, as this search shares marked similarities with those of the Gestapo in old war movies. Our familiar senior agent exits Milonja's small living room, which leaves Milovan with two young BIA drones to assist. He storms into the kitchen, opening cabinets and drawers; lifts a pot lid from the stove, and recoils in disgust from some formerly edible substance. He quickly replaces the lid and scans the room. His attention is drawn to a notepad magnetically attached to the refrigerator, but it contains nothing but the phone number for a kebab takeaway joint. Disappointed, he opens the fridge, takes out a bottle of Jelen beer, sets its top against the edge of the counter, and forcefully slams the cap off the bottle. Furious and thirsty in equal measure, he takes several generous swigs before hurling the bottle at a wall clock. Glass shrapnel explodes from the boozy explosion, and the clock shatters into countless pieces with a deafening crash. Milovan materialises at the door, witness to the carnage in the kitchen—and also to his superior, who is seated at the dining table, urgently massaging his temples. Torn between the urge to say something and fear of the potential reaction, Milovan settles on hovering awkwardly a couple paces away.

"Do you have any aspirin, Milovan?"

"I don't think so."

"You don't think so? Do me a favour and send one of your drones to get me some. I'm falling apart."

Milovan moves instantly to follow his orders, but he's interrupted by the doorbell. He checks the peephole, and then opens the door to a scowling older lady in a housecoat and slippers. Undeterred by his mammoth size, she springs at the unsuspecting security agent, and beats him across the face and shoulders.

"You thieving bastards! You won't forget me soon, eh!? The audacity! Burglary in broad daylight!"

A bewildered Milovan takes a couple steps back. He raises his arms in defence but, becoming frustrated, then shoves his hands into his pockets instead and resigns himself to her fury. The behemoth's colleagues are cracking up in the background, and it's hard to blame them.

That her blows have absolutely no effect, and that Milovan has the bandwidth to send someone off to the pharmacy for his superior's painkillers, these things might deter some assailants. Not this fiery old lady, however.

The agent observes her from his towering height with evident pity, but makes no attempt to calm her. The lady, increasingly out of breath and her pace slackening, continues her assault, righteous anger seeming to cloud all reason. She might have collapsed if the hard, older security agent hadn't reappeared and escorted her into the kitchen to sit. He pours her a glass of water and sets it before her, then leans his forehead against the window pane and whistles some tune. (A football anthem?) Milovan soon enters the kitchen himself to confer with his senior colleague, but the latter shoos him out with an abrupt gesture and continues to whistle.

"You thieving... bastards... Do you even know... whose flat... you came... to rob?" The agent hears the lady behind him, her voice still ragged.

The fed-up, grizzled BIA agent squeezes his eyes shut, not in the mood to be berated, especially not by some crazy old woman. For a moment, he even contemplates the satisfaction of taking her out. Bullet to the forehead. He reaches for the gun at his waist, but then thinks better of it and tosses his official badge onto the table in front of her. At first, she pretends not to care and continues to rant, but her eyes keep darting to the intriguing leather object. Eventually, she picks it up, revealing a badge with some emblem. However, she seems unable to make out the name *Marjan Kostreš*, even holding the badge at the very end of her fingertips, arms painfully extended.

"It's no use; I didn't bring my glasses."

"BIA, ma'am."

"Excuse me?"

"The Security-Intelligence Agency!!"

"One more time, dear?"

"People's Protection Department,[1] you deaf old bat! Your esteemed comrade-neighbour has been engaged in anti-state activities for some time now, and he's currently a fugitive from justice."

"Who?! Milonja Šoškić? Anti-state activities? What have you been smoking!? You must be out of your minds."

Agent Kostreš's skin itches with rage, and he instinctively reaches back for his gun. This time, however, Milovan appears to save the day, painkiller-in-hand. Knocking the pill back without water, Kostreš claps his younger colleague on the shoulder in lieu of verbal gratitude.

"So, Milovan, did we find anything?"

Milovan shakes his head in resignation. From the side, the old woman interjects that Milonja will be back any moment now, and will surely make them rue their interference in their building's affairs.

---

1. The Odeljenje za zaštitu naroda, Yugoslavia's original secret police agency and the predecessor of the BIA.

"I swear to God, Milovan, I'll smack her right in her face. Get her out of here," Kostreš fumes through gritted teeth and steps through a room which has, in these few brief minutes, descended into total chaos.

If a grenade had exploded here minutes ago, it couldn't have been much worse. In the background, we hear the indomitable old lady screaming and shouting as Milovan guides her back to her apartment. Meanwhile, Kostreš watches disdainfully from the side as the two nameless agents rummage haphazardly through heaps of irrelevant junk. Although he ought to reprimand them, the aspirin hasn't kicked in yet and he lacks the energy for sustained disciplinary action. Turning away from his bumbling goons, Kostreš spies a couple of photos sticking out from between the pages of a book lying on the floor. Bending down to examine them, he quickly realises that every photograph captures the same day, at the same place—a monastery—with the same two smiling figures: Inspector Milonja Šoškić and an unknown Serbian Orthodox monk. We exchange nervous glances, for the monk in the photograph is, in fact, entirely known to us. An excitable youth in our company moves to speak, but is swiftly silenced from all corners. Milovan soon re-enters the room, and Kostreš immediately flings the photos in his face: "Do you know where this is?"

Milovan knits his brow, and spins the wheels of cogitation. He doesn't want to suffer the consequences of an uninformed guess, but neither does he relish a new opportunity to prove his uselessness. Finally, the younger security agent lands on: "I don't know. I believe it's a monastery of some sort."

Kostreš is dumbfounded. He stares at Milovan, trying to process this latest statement with apparent difficulty. He'd be far less repulsed by some tasteless joke, which he would, at least, understand. Instead, he's left maddeningly perplexed by the molasses-slowness of his colleague's deductive skills. Turning the monastery photos over in his hands, he wonders when the BIA became a haven for dense imbeciles.

"Really? I wonder how you figured that out?" Kostreš asks, voice dripping with irony. The sarcasm, however, sails over Milovan's head, and the younger agent begins to earnestly elaborate on the steeple visible in the background. But the veteran agent cuts him off:

"I know that, Gvozdenović—I'm not blind! Idiot! I see that it's a monastery, but which one? Does either of you know?"

"Yes! It's Banjska! One of the many endowments of Milutin, the Saint King of Serbia!" one of the two rookies exclaims, having, it would seem, waited his entire life to share this knowledge.

"Are you sure?" Milovan asks, sceptical.

"One hundred percent. I was there last year. The monk in the picture is the abbot, Father Stefan."

"See, Milovan? There's more to life than just the football," Kostreš chides him in a fatherly tone. "What was your name, kid?"

"Ubović," the young agent replies.

"Ubović? Any relation to Mita? He was the president of the Bar Association, for a year or two."

"That's my uncle."

"Really?"

"Yes."

"Good for you, Ubović! Now tell me, for the love of God, where is this monastery?"

"In Kosovo, actually. Just across the border."

"OK, perfect! Would you be able to take Milovan along to acquaint him with our proud heritage, show him there are grounds more sacred even than Marakana?[2] And, while you're at it, check around for a couple fugitives."

"Oh! You mean... right now?" Kostreš might as well have told him that Christmas was cancelled.

"You're right, Ubović, it's almost time for your bedtime story—yes, *of course right now!* A free day trip, the company pays, what's your concern?"

"That's really nice of course, but I'm not sure if I can..."

"Of course you can, Ubović. I've no energy left for games!"

"Yes sir, of course sir. The thing is, I'd promised my girlfriend I'd visit her. I'm actually *already* late, so..."

The expression on Kostreš's face resembles a smile as described by one who has only a theoretical acquaintance with happiness, his glare cold and metallic.

---

2. Nickname for the home grounds of Belgrade's iconic Red Star football club, taken from Rio de Janeiro's Maracanã Stadium.

"Fair play, Ubović. I'm sure they'll be happy to wait for you. Maybe call the monastery though, just to check? If they pick up themselves, go ahead and ask them to wait a couple of days—you're busy after all! No reason to limit yourself to just the first half of the *Kama Sutra*, right?"

"No no it's not like that with us, it's just—"

"I get it, young man! The security-intelligence administration sincerely requests all enemies of state to suspend hostile activities because, you see, Ubović has some immovable love-making on his agenda."

"I..."

"Shut up and listen, rook: When I joined the BIA in '91, my boss was the legendary Jova Somborac. On the very first day, he sat me down and said, 'Kid, if you're not ready to show up here in the middle of the night, even if you're in the middle of making love to the most beautiful woman in Ribarac, you better ask your dad to get you a job someplace else.' And, as you see, Ubović, I'm still here because, thanks to Major Somborac, I realised that our work is critical and must never be compromised. Remember, young man: You'll have many women in your life, but only one motherland—and you must protect her! Have you heard the saying, Ubović, that 'Serbia is eternal as long as her children remain loyal'?

The rookie agent dejectedly studies the floor. His conversion to the cause remains incomplete, and thoughts simmer which threaten to boil over. Milovan swings to Ubović's rescue however, clapping him reassuringly on the shoulder; an invitation-order to follow him out of Milonja's apartment. For his part, Kostreš tosses some car keys at Ubović.

"Take my Škoda. You'll get there faster."

For several tense seconds, Ubović stares impotently at the keys, before closing his fingers over them and retreating from the apartment with Milovan in tow. Kostreš observes his subordinates with a calm gaze and a satisfied smile which is undeniably, almost cinematically, villainous.

"Like Ralph Fiennes as the Nazi in *Schindler's List*!" whispers a young woman among us. An older gentleman adds, "Or Rade Marković as Miloje in *Majstori, majstori*."

Marjan Kostreš slowly turns to face us, meeting our eyes directly and breaking into mirthless laughter. He has clearly heard this entire whispered exchange. An overpowering wave of unease engulfs us all; it quickly becomes so unbearable that we beat a hasty exit into the next chapter.

25

IN THE ER WAITING area, we are reunited with the True Creators. Their fighting spirit all but extinguished, the writers share a deep, and very visible, fatigue. Đorđe Smolović, torn and tattered, wounded and dirty, limps up and down the corridor, and grumbles aimlessly to himself. He's frustrated by the wait time and, although he insists that *the waiting itself isn't the issue*, he simply cannot understand why the nurse on duty refuses to call Dr. Koprivica and inform him that Đorđe Smolović is in the waiting area. The three other Creators are seated, in varying states of disengagement from Đorđe's dispute. More specifically, Moca and Borojević have nodded off on each other's shoulders, while Voja scrolls furiously and, we think, aimlessly through his phone. Our protagonist's drooping eyes and nodding head betray his own exhaustion. After every nod, Voja darts a fierce glance around the room, to check whether anyone has caught his moment of vulnerability.

"Sir! How many times must I repeat that I won't call Dr Koprivica for you? You can very well call him yourself," the duty nurse addresses Đorđe with a polite but raised voice.

"Well, I would if I could! But I've lost my phone. Obviously. Just look at the state I'm in, for heaven's sake!"

We join the duty nurse in appraising the once-stately author's appearance, and concede that he's a sight to behold. Had we not witnessed the events that led Đorđe to the ER, we might imagine him recently returned from a graduation formal he attended in 1974, having spent the intervening years lost in a haunted forest along with his classmates. In that decades-long struggle for survival, bearing deep scars—both physical and emotional—from conflicts, competition, regular run-ins with spirits and otherworldly apparitions, and the odd cannibalistic encounter, Đorđe Smolović emerged as the ultimate victor. Granted, it's difficult to imagine the Đorđe before us having been especially victorious in...anything... But the haunted forest scenario is already a decent feat of imagination in and of itself.

"Smolović!" A hoarse alto voice echoes from the doorway, following a discomfited-looking man wearing work clothes and a patch over his right eye.

Đorđe leaps up but a sharp pain in his leg cautions against overexertion.

"Smolović!" The voice rings out, even louder this time.

"I'm here! Here!" he shouts, hurrying as best he can.

On the faces of the other ER patients, we read—between the confusion and mild revulsion—an absolute readiness to rush the door at the first hint of their own names being read, wounded poets be damned. Therefore, the struggling Đorđe shouts again:

"I'm...! Coming...!"

And indeed, he makes it. By the skin of his teeth. The operatic nurse was already gathering breath for the next patient but, upon seeing the ragged Smolović at the door, instead exclaims:

"Good Lord! What happened to you?" Đorđe shuts the door in our faces but, through it, we can just about discern the shape of a pretty fantastic story. Apparently, somewhere near Spens, Đorđe defended an innocent maiden from a group of thuggish young men. He had just finished incapacitating them when, in a last-ditch effort, one of the scoundrels unleashed a massive Doberman. We assume that the doctor asks if he's informed the police because, after Đorđe says 'No,' he immediately tells the duty nurse:

"Anđela, get the Novi Sad PD down here to deal with Mr Smolović."

After a short spell, four uniformed police officers walk into the ER. Three of them scan the scene while the fourth cautiously approaches the slumping True Creators, while casting periodic glances down at his phone. He dials a number, listens for a ring—which comes about one second later—and then pulls the phone away from his ear. He tracks the ringtone to a woman's purse beside our drowsy protagonist. The officer's suspicions are confirmed. He gestures to his colleagues, who draw their guns. Moments later, our True Creators are completely surrounded by cops with guns aimed at them, and the only saving grace is that, for this blissful moment, they are entirely unaware of it.

As the waiting room quickly drains of patients with better places to be, the only sound is Maja's iPhone, still ringing too quietly to awaken the exhausted writers. Voja's head droops to his shoulder, and his bowler droops to his nose. Realising that they might be in for a long wait otherwise, one of the cops cautiously closes the distance between him and the True Creators.

He's just a step away from Voja's chair, and a finger's breadth from the strap of Maja's purse, when the ringtone cuts out. Voja's bowler falls off and rolls on the floor. His head follows the hat, and his whole body follows the head. With a sudden jolt, he leaps back up, doing his best to dismiss a vague suspicion that all is not entirely right with the Emergency Room. He removes his glasses to see if the lenses are intact and, when he replaces them a moment later, is nonplussed by the scene which greets him. Out of instinct more than reason—Voja rather assumes he's dreaming at this point—he raises his hands above his head, palms facing outward. When one of the cops advances briskly to clap cuffs around his wrists, however, our hero reluctantly accepts that he must be awake.

"You are under arrest," the officer says, dispensing with any remaining confusion on the matter. "Are these two with you?" Voja's mind remains a void of bafflement. Momentarily, and uncharacteristically, bereft for words, our protagonist nods mutely. When he recovers the power of speech, he earnestly conveys that there's been a deeply unfortunate misunderstanding, and that all of them—cops and Creators alike—are on the same side.

"We aren't criminals! We are authors whose works your children will study in Serbian language classes one day. We are the architects of some of the most refined literary achievements ever committed to the Serbian tongue. We are the True Creators, those who stand against servile mediocrity in the face of humiliation; we are—"

"True creators, servile mediocrity, we get it, boss!" interrupts one of the policemen, grabbing Voja's arm and leading him towards the exit. His colleagues round up Borojević and Moca, who, being handcuffed after Voja, are behind the curve in comprehending their abrupt change of circumstances.

"WAIT!" The duty nurse, who had been sheltering from the unpleasantness, shoots out from under her desk and hands Maja's purse to the cops.

Along with the assembled hospital staff and patients, we watch in sombre silence as a quorum of the Club of True Creators is piled into two black SUVs. The vehicles grumble reluctantly to life and then skid off in the direction of the Novi Sad PD municipal detention centre. After this, the ER waiting room returns to business as usual, and we're once again faced with a dilemma: though some of us suggest that resting a spell and waiting for Đorđe's discharge, most of us believe, considering the extent and nature of his injuries, that this might constitute a long wait. Thus, we resolve to head back to the monastery and check in for any updates.

26

"ULTIMATELY, IT'S JUST A matter of fact. We are the best, smartest, most beautiful, and most peaceful nation in the history of civilization, always on the side of truth and justice. Miroslav, Miroljub, Mirjana, Mirko, Vladimir—our children are christened with peace, and our priests are its guardians.[1] Serbians are the most peaceful people on earth: and that is why they hate us. We are more peaceful than Lennon, the truest peacemakers. Our greatest cause, and the cause for which we will proudly sacrifice, is the cause of peace. Because without peace, there is no Serbia.

"We can coexist peacefully with anyone...except for 'them,' 'them,' 'them,' 'them,' and 'them'—our immortal enemies, the scum on the heel of civilization, living, walking shit. The destabilising forces for whom hatred is in their very nature. And let the entire universe hear and remember: there can *be* no peace until we've settled our borders with "them," once and for all." Abbot Stefan, having worked himself up into a frenzy, exhales several centuries of inter-ethnic tension from his diaphragm.

---

1. mir = peace

"So, tell me: how *senseless*, how just plain *stupid*, must one be to think that that is the solution? 'Settle borders?' Give me a break. Can we please just live in reality!?"

We don't know precisely when or how this socio-political exegesis began, but we see that the breakfast table is full, the meal is well under way, and that our riled-up priest shows no signs of imminently reaching a conclusion.

"Ah, the human mind is such a beautiful enigma. Our people constitute living proof that a nation can suffer from psychosocial complexes deeper than any one individual. Mile, do you remember that kid Koruga who did regular high school and the music academy at the same time?" Milonja nods, mouth full of toast. "Guy thought he was a genius, a cross between Jethro Tull and Nikola Tesla. And you know what? He might damn well have been, if he hadn't spent so much time gazing into the well of his own genius.

"But he could never find a skilled musician to follow his chaotic rock symphonies. Eventually, he settled for his flautist sister and his dad playing on an old Casio. Back then, one couldn't find a incompetent drummer in Novi Sad, let alone a proficient one, so Koruga laid down the percussion himself with a drum machine. And, you know, the three of them built a career of sorts, albeit to the obvious displeasure of the wider listening public. They played on for years, to literally dozens of people, powered purely by spite. I guarantee there was no joy in the experience. In the end, Koruga ditched them both and tried to make it on his own as a singer-songwriter, but his only album was a joke. Totally unlistenable."

"Who's this Koruga? I assume I should have heard of him," Nataša says just before taking a final bite of toast and washing it down with orange juice.

Abbot Stefan raises an eyebrow. "You absolutely should *not* have heard of him. The most anonymous rock star in history. Less famous than Đorđe David,[2] if that's possible. Why would you know him?"

"But wait, Stevo, what happened to the guy in the end? How did things end up for him?" Milonja rejoins, polishing off his own plate.

"What, Koruga? Oh, he killed himself. What else? Years ago. I was still back in Kovilj."

A brief pause follows, during which we try to work out what (if any) moral might be gleaned from Koruga's tragic tale. Judging by the sea of blank faces, however, it seems that Father Stefan's parable defies easy analysis. The priest, perhaps sensing this, offers an assist:

"Better someone who admits their flaws and works to improve, than one who boasts of their own perfection."

While this sentence echoes in our minds, we envision it engraved—many decades hence—on the tombstone of Banjska's

---

2. Vocalist and actor who has belonged to a number of Yugoslav and Serbian rock bands, among them Generacija 5, Griva, Ciklon, Garavi Sokak, and Death Saw.

abbot. A tranquil silence descends on the dining room, and a blissful serenity fills the air.

Then, from Milonja: "I've decided to call Vuletić."

The Abbot stops chewing for a moment and looks at his friend as if he's finally, irrevocably, lost it. "*Vuletić?*"

Milonja nods.

"You really mean your Vuletić? Mister Deputy General Prosecutor Vuletić?"

"Yes, I talked with Nataša and..."

"*That* Vuletić? Your old pal from university who has let you down, literally, countless times? The same Vuletić with whom you cut ties permanently, what, has it already been fifteen years...?"

"I know, Stevo, but..."

"*Vuletić?* That leech and sycophant who managed to cast back every big fish you caught for him? Not only caught, but cleaned and served up fried with a side of coleslaw. No, I refuse to believe it. Please, Mile, tell me you're joking."

Milonja says nothing, most especially not that he's joking. He remains silent, looking at Nataša, who looks an unspoken question over at him.

"All right, all of that is true," Milonja concedes, "But it's not like we've got an embarrassment of options. I'm sure Vule won't betray us. At worst he'll say, 'Milonja, you're an insane old man, I won't do it, let's pretend this conversation never happened.' But he won't turn us over, no chance. According to article three of the 2005 Law for the Protection of Participants in Criminal Proceedings..."

"What are you...? Even...? Lord protect us—please don't tell me you're as naïve as that. Milonja," the priest's eyes shimmer, "I'm honestly begging you."

Milonja observes first his friend and then Nataša before standing up in resignation and heading for the door. Reaching the threshold, he pauses just long enough to lob back at Abbot Stefan.

"You're right, Stevo, I've been foolish and naïve all my life. But you're not much better than I am, if you think we're safe here. We've run out of time."

After the passage of a few hushed and heavy moments, Nataša rises abruptly and begins clearing dirty dishes and left-overs from the table. The abbot crosses himself and continues to eat from his plate. The dining room door creaks open just enough for Milonja to poke his head through and add, "Actually, I wouldn't be surprised if they're already on their way."

27

BEHIND THE WHEEL OF Kostreš's Škoda, Ubović traces a winding road. The rookie BIA agent tries to concentrate on an old folk song warbling from the radio, but is mostly listening to his colleague Milovan, who says to him:

"Look, kid, you understand how screwed we are if Kostreš finds out that we didn't get off until five. You and your girlfriend..."

"Of course I do, Milovan. I coached her exactly what to say if he calls to check."

"Not 'if,' but 'when.' I know him, and he will absolutely call."

"How would he even have her phone number?" Scepticism fights a losing match with anxiety across Ubović's face.

"I'm not even sure, but I do know he'll call her. The guy is a certified dickhead."

"And if he calls *me*...I should tell him we're near the border?"

"Right."

A slow-moving tractor takes up nearly two full lanes ahead of them; Ubović passes it on the left shoulder. "Did you manage to get some sleep?"

"No, but I popped two guarana pills and I have another one in reserve."

"OK, let me know if you feel sleepy."

"All right."

While they were talking, the folk music on the radio was replaced by the news. And the news, as usual, isn't very good. The hulking security agent curses under his breath, and switches quickly to another station, where the music, improbably, seems even worse to our ears than the news had been. But not to Milovan's ears apparently, as he sits back a little and even begins to hum along.

"*You're a real lady, lady-dee-dee-dee / Out on the floor-oor-oor-oor!*"

God is undoubtedly just, thinks Ubović. For, though Milovan is blessed with nearly superhuman strength, he is painfully deficient of any musical sense. His younger colleague throws him a pitying glance. As pity turns to irritation, however, the young agent attempts to revive the conversation:

"So, Milovan. Did you see that story about the string of mysterious deaths?"

He nods minimally in acknowledgment and continues with his off-key singing. The topic has failed to arouse interest. Undeterred, Ubović tries again: "It's all very odd, isn't it?"

"Yes," Milovan replies tersely, and continues:

"*I sawwwww her at the market*

Asked: 'What you looking fo-o-or?'

She said, 'Just here for a kiwi, don't get hot.'

But you've got that booty, how could I not?

I won't disappoint, girl. Give me a shot..."

"And what do you think...?" Ubović valiantly tries to form some further words, but Milovan places a finger on his lips and turns up the radio:

"Listen to this! This is brilliant:

"*So what! So what! I'm a hooligan!*

Loudly I chant, go Serbia! Serbia!

Champion to champion, brothers in arms..."

By this point, we can only assume that Ubović's thoughts have turned towards self-harm. A few tortured moments pass before the rookie's mobile phone brings him back to earth. As expected, the groggy voice of a recently awakened Marjan Kostreš drips down the speaker:

"Ubović. Have you caught them? Where are you?"

"Haven't caught them yet. We're near the Kosovo border. We hit some traffic on the road."

"Traffic? I see. Where are you, exactly?"

"Well... we're right... here..."

Milovan, attempting an assist, gestures vaguely and waves his hand around. This looks to be as unhelpful to Ubović as it was to us.

"At the foot of Kopaonik," the younger agent says with phoney confidence. "We've already passed Raška."

"Are you sure about that, Ubović? Because, according to Milovan's phone location, you're not even past Ljig." Milovan slaps his forehead, realising he forgot to...

"Ljig?" Ubović tries, "Isn't that near Kopaonik?"

"Don't play the fool; I know you aren't one. Where is Milovan? Driving?"

Milovan slams his eyelids shut in a flash of terror and affects an abrupt, rigid slumber. His suddenly bereft chauffeur stammers: "No... er, he's asleep... I'm driving... he's asleep."

"Get serious, Ubović, for the love of God! Now, listen to me—you too, Gvozdenović! Floor it and make sure you're back to Novi Sad by nightfall. Capiche?!"

"But...Marjan, what if they aren't there?" Milovan timidly asks.

"If you don't find them, Milovan...then you're fucked. Don't bother coming back."

The call ends.

If the sudden tension filling the car could be measured by a gauge on its dashboard, the needle would have leapt to its most clockwise extremity.

Milovan instructs his younger colleague to pull over at the earliest opportunity so that they can switch places. When they do so, the Škoda's new driver slams the accelerator, the agency car skidding and screeching back onto the highway. However, since the majority of us didn't sign up for the *Fast and Furious*, we decide to end this chapter—with immediate effect.

28

IN AN ANONYMOUS DETENTION unit of the Novi Sad central police station, three True Creators face perhaps their most challenging moment yet—disunited and defeated, both spiritually and physically, hungry, thirsty, fatigued, unkempt. Although they're not even on neighbouring benches, Voja hears Borojević muttering under his breath. He doesn't need to catch every word to know that he is the subject of the muttering. Although irritated, our protagonist is much too depleted for further confrontation.

Instead, Voja pulls a pen and pad from his overcoat and plunges nose-first into the creative process, which is truly captivating. Admirable, even. Several of us express amazement at Voja's writerly passion, which remains undimmed under even these oppressive conditions. Any of us who had remained unclear on the key distinction between the True Creators and the run-of-the-mill ones, is unclear no longer. Only the most sophisticated and versatile writer can pull inspiration from a vacuum. Only the most exceptional artist is fueled by such a powerful and consistent creative flame. Only the purest genius can transcend ego for the perfection of his own work. Only the Truest Creators can transform and elevate us, stealing us away from our grim individual realities to the exalted realm of universal insight, leading us beyond the metaphysical and all the way back to the physical, with the promise of solace and hope...

Republic of Serbia
Ministry of Internal Affairs
To: Minister Aleksandar Galić (Personal)

REQUEST

Honourable Minister, whereas the arrest of myself and my colleagues from the Club of True Creators is the result of a concerted attack by foreign embassies, agencies, and local NGO activists, I hereby request that we be released at the earliest possible opportunity, with preference for the immediate. These circumstances constitute a terrible misunderstanding, as well as a deliberate obfuscation of reality which has, in a mere 48 hours, made a culprit of the victim, and a victim of the culprit.

It is my sincere wish that this shameful imprisonment of the Novi Sad's most distinguished literary figures, which is an unprecedented stain on Serbia's history, will conclude before news of our arrest reaches the Association of Writers of Serbia, the wider media, and the public at large. Because, rest assured, in that event, you will face an overwhelming surge of dissatisfaction, and massive protests in the squares and streets of our cities.

Vojislav Počuča

Writer
Songwriter
Founder, Club of True Creators

"Guard! Guard!" Voja calls, rapping his pen against the bars. "Sir! Hey there!"

Although no guard comes, Voja's persistence in the effort cannot be faulted. "He probably took a break. Cigarette maybe," Moca speculates.

"And what about you, Vojo? Feel like a breather? I don't know what you're up to but, I have to say, I think you've done enough at this point," Borojević finally gives voice to frustrations that have been simmering since the cornfield.

Voja glares contemptuously at him and retorts:

"Oh really, Boro? I'm the one to blame, huh? I'm the one at fault when they tried to ASSASSINATE me, huh? Is that it? Well, I'll take that blame! It means I'm the biggest thorn in their side!"

"You, Vojo?"

"Of course, me! Who did they go for first, you or me?"

"Don't be ridiculous. Moco, come on, talk some sense into him. It always seems like I'm the one..."

"I don't know, Boro," Moca cuts him off. "None of this makes sense to me. I don't understand who's to blame, how we ended up in this mess, or honestly much of what's happened at all in the last couple days.

"Main thing I know is, I'm starving and, if they don't feed us soon, I'm going to snap and assassinate both of you."

Moca's words have a transformative effect on the other two Creators—some harrowing memory of an earlier hunger-induced fury no doubt. Voja begins to call out even more urgently for the officer on duty, and this time Borojević joins him. Their voices have grown quite hoarse by the time a very weary-looking guard finally shows up.

"What the hell do you want?"

Borojević and Voja start to talk at once, but the latter, raising his voice, quickly gets the upper hand. He urgently informs the guard that they must be fed as soon as possible, lest their colleague suffer a 'gastro-hysterical' episode. He quickly clarifies that this is a medical diagnosis, not a passing whim, and concludes with a final plea for haste, warning of dire, if somewhat amorphous, consequences. He also hands over the REQUEST, scrawled over two torn-out pages from his notebook, and asks that this be delivered to the Ministry posthaste. The guard looks at him blankly, glances at the other Creators, stuffs the pages in his pocket, and leaves without a word. Borojević calls after him to add that he barely knows the other two, and he wishes to speak to his lawyer. The guard pays him no mind, but does return a minute later with three cans of spam and a loaf of bread.

"All right fellas, hurry up with this. The detectives are waiting for you downstairs. Call out when you're done."

Incredible. They pounce on the food so eagerly that we scarcely have time to make room for the gluttonous orgy. And then, just like that, they're already calling for the guard. He reappears, astonished at the disappearing act. He gives them cleanup instructions, unlocks the cell, and tells them to leave single file. He silences them sternly as they burst from the cell, forestalling any further claims of conspiracy and misunderstanding. As the four figures slowly transform into silhouettes and are swallowed by the dark corridor, we hear the officer's words of consolation:

"Life is *all* one damn big misunderstanding. Take me: I stopped the biggest dealer in Novi Sad this morning with two kilos of heroin in his trunk, and now I'm here serving you spam. Unbelievable!"

29

On the concrete pathway leading away from the main complex of the Provincial Hospital, we find Marjan Kostreš pushing his longtime colleague and friend, Rajko Pešut, in a wheelchair. Pešut has just been discharged from hospital treatment, but his punch-drunk gaze, eyes darting enthusiastically but aimlessly, demonstrate that his recovery is primarily physical. Kostreš is visibly frustrated by his friend's amnesia, his every attempt at conversation fizzling on impact.

"Hold up, Rale, you can't remember *anything?* Not even when we got drunk at Beza's place last month, and Milovan carried you all the way home on a dare?"

Although Pešut doesn't respond, his blank expression says it all.

"He carried you all the way from Štrand...to...? Come on, buddy, I'm sure you know where you live..."

Despite a visible mental effort, Pešut can only shake his head helplessly from side to side.

"Well, how about Ljubljana?! Don't tell me you've forgotten the time when Sgt Prostran barged into the guardhouse at two in the morning, drunk off his face, but there was no one there because the duty guard had taken the night off with some girl soldier in Pinca?"

"I... remember only... my grandmother making me *pofezne*. "[1]

"Just your grandma and 'pofezne'?"

Pešut tries to reply but the words won't come. He's on the verge of tears. He's forced to look down, lips pressed together, assenting with the barest of nods.

"Damn it, Rajko! As if I needed another child in my life!" Kostreš pulls his mobile from his pocket, checks the time, and realises that Milovan and Ubović should have contacted him by now. He contemplates checking in on them but decides instead to give them another half-hour. He's worried about Rajko. He is, at the moment, clearly unfit for independent living. Kostreš wonders if he should find his friend a homecare worker for the time being, or even take him in himself. At least until his memory has partially returned or, God forbid, he's relearnt everything from scratch. After some deep reflection, Kostreš concludes neither option is ideal.

First, he's never been one to live with a roommate. The mere idea of sharing personal space has always been anathema to him. He recalls briefly the total disaster in which all three of his attempts at amorous cohabitation had ended.

---

1. Fried savoury dumplings, a regional term, which seems unfamiliar to Marjan.

Secondly, and worse, Pešut has always had a strong predatory streak. Two alleged incidents of assaulting female fellow officers, which the court never proved, and who-knows-how-many rapes during the war, are reason enough not to expose him to any unnecessary female contact. Hiring a live-in homecare worker would almost certainly do that. Kostreš pulls the wheelchair to an abrupt stop by a bench, lighting a cigarette and ruminating further on Pešut's future. Should he check on those goons yet? He checks the time but it's still only been...

"Marjan!" With a curious mix of joy and exhaustion in his voice, Đorđe Smolović greets the veteran security agent. It's difficult to imagine an acquaintance from happier days recognizing Đorđe in his current state. Drawing the tobacco smoke deep into his lungs, Kostreš eyes the oddly elongated figure looming over him, and tries to ascertain its identity. The many bandages give the old man a mummified appearance. In the end, it's no use: the stranger will have to introduce himself:

"It's me, damn it! Smolović! Đorđe Smolović!"

"Đorđe?! What the hell happened to you? You're a...well, a mess!"

"Honestly... don't even ask."

"What do you mean, 'don't ask'? Tell me, man, don't leave me hanging..."

"All right, all right. As you know, those paragons of political correctness..."

"Who?"

"You know, those untalented Euro-chauvinists and propagandist hacks who've been polluting our True Creative Essence for years."

"Hold on, hold on," Kostreš holds up a hand, completely lost. "Who's doing what now? I need more here."

"In short: the cultural war that's been simmering for thirty years in our beloved Serbia finally erupted yesterday."

"You're kidding, Đorđe! Tell me everything; I'm genuinely very curious. What happened? How did it start?"

"You won't believe it, Marjan. It actually started when my friend Voja, from our Club of True Creators, left an innocent comment on a Facebook post by the infamous Nataša Žarković."

"*What?!*"

"You've definitely heard of her; we've talked about her a hundred times. If I understood Voja correctly—I abstain from social media myself—she wrote an unhinged attack on how the Ministry of Culture has distributed prize funds over the past few years. As you know, I often serve on those committees. I have no clue why she's bringing it up now in September, when the results were announced at the end of April. But, that's beside the point. If I remember correctly, Voja replied back on the Facebook post that she should stand to attention when uttering the names of the committee members, whose artistic stature and contributions to the motherland demand respect, not petty accusations. I think he also called her a self-loathing traitor who operates from a position of constant comfort and privilege, bankrolled by foreign millionaires."

"And then?"

Though he puts on an admirable show of curiosity, Kostreš has clearly worked out the rest of the story, and is ready for it to end.

"And *then*, Marjan," Đorđe continues, "night before last, she hops into her shitty red car and tries to flatten Voja at point blank range. Fortunately, some other guy pops out in front of him, and she hits him instead."

"No way," Kostreš grimaces. "Do you happen to know who that unlucky fellow was?"

"Exactly! We had to respond," Đorđe blithely continues. "The Club of True Creators held an extraordinary conference at which we decided to avenge this assault decisively and without mercy."

"It got heated, I can tell."

Đorđe doesn't appreciate this sarcastic remark. He responds petulantly that his injuries are mere scratches compared to those inflicted upon the Club's adversaries. In reply, Kostreš manages to express some token admiration for the True Creators. Still, he raises a hand, places a finger over the author's lips. The agent studies Đorđe's bandaged face intently before saying:

"Tell me, Đorđe, do you ever wish you were normal?"

"I'm sorry, Marjan, I don't underst—"

"No, *I* don't understand. Why would you get involved in a stupid mess like this without talking to your friend in the *Security-Intelligence Administration?*"

"But Marjan..."

"Shut up, you IDIOT! Your Club of True Creators defending the homeland? Ridiculous! Why would you even imagine that someone would try to kill your Voja over some damn internet comment?"

Đorđe reflects for a moment before conceding, "All right, I confess Nataša's reaction might have been disproportionate. But lately, everyone has been so tense, Marjan. I wouldn't doubt anything. Honestly, it's no surprise that this is where we ended up, because the truth is—"

"The truth, Đorđe, is that Nataša Žarković hit the exact person she intended to hit. This man right here, Rajko Pešut, my colleague and friend. The one in a wheelchair. The one who, after Žarković knocked him to the ground, lost all his memory."

Đorđe is now, understandably, at a loss for words. He wriggles in discomfort, while Pešut, who has been seated inertly this whole time, finally has a contribution since, actually, he does remember something: his grandmother's *pofezne*.

"Oh, right, the 'pofezne!' How could I ever forget?!" exclaims Kostreš, before leaning in to Đorđe so as not to raise his voice. "Listen to me, pal. I don't know how you'll get out of this mess, and frankly, I could not care less."

"Marjan, please, I haven't even finished explaining..."

"You didn't hear me, Smolović. I could not *fucking* care less."

Đorđe accepts that any further attempt would only damage his case, so he decides to give up, hesitating even to say goodbye. He tentatively offers Kostreš his hand but, when the agent affects not to see it, Đorđe has no choice but to instead pat Pešut on the shoulder and limp away toward the taxi stand. The two old BIA agents are left sitting opposite each other, regarding each other in silence until, suddenly, Kostreš leaps off the bench as if stung in the rear.

First, he rings Milovan and paces nervously while waiting for him to pick up. When there's no response, he tries Ubović, whereupon a pleasant female voice informs him that the mobile subscriber he is trying to reach is regrettably unavailable. Kostreš runs several paces out, and furiously kicks an empty beer can several metres in the air. Returning to the bench, he takes a couple of restorative breaths and looks at the depleted Pešut.

"So, what now, Rale?"

Pešut merely shrugs blankly and looks away. Kostreš lowers himself, grasps his friend's shoulders, and gives him a pat on the knee. "I hope you're hungry, boss. Lets go to mine and fix you up some *pofezne*."

30

NATAŠA'S THREE DOGS ARE already patiently seated in the back of the red Renault 4, their tails wagging with happiness as their mistress joins them in the passenger seat. Having just bid their farewells to the young monks of the Banjska Monastery and their abbot, Nataša and her dogs are now waiting only for Milonja to do the same.

"Mile, I'm so worried you're making a mistake. Please reconsider. How can you trust Vuletić?"

"Come on, Stevo, not this again," Milonja implores. "Like I said, the security agents are certainly already on their way. This thing with Vuletić, we don't have a choice. I'm not being...capricious..."

Father Stefan looks ready to say more but chooses to hold his silence. Instead, he takes Milonja's face in his hands, cherishing it as if it were the Holy Grail, and looks directly into his eyes with a deep, shimmering gaze. He hugs him, abruptly and fiercely, which Milonja reciprocates. Among our group, a shaggy-haired painter looks on and wishes he had the tools to commit this touching scene immortally to canvas.

"Stevo, it's time. Thank you for everything."

"Go, then, go, safe travels, and may the Lord protect you. Please, send word when you're safe."

Taking his leave at last, Milonja gets into the car, and Father Stefan calls out with a mischievous grin, "And Mile, if you decide to get married for a fifth time...*please* let us host the wedding here?"

A reddening Milonja plays at being deaf, starts the car, and glances at Nataša, who suppresses a smile. The monks and abbot wave together as the Renault 4 pulls away from the monastery grounds. A bell tolls in the distance and, through the rearview mirror, the two travellers can see the abbot of Banjska monastery praying earnestly for their safety.

31

THE THREE TRUE CREATORS are returned to their cell following an initial hearing. They look deeply unhappy—to be expected, we suppose. Several minutes into a long, strained silence, Voja clears his throat and announces:

"I propose that the Club of True Creators establish a new award. It would be given annually, recognizing exceptional artistic potential and contribution to culture. In addition to an honorary plaque, it would also grant membership to the Club. What do you think?"

The response is subarctic. In fact, judging by their blank stares, the other Creators seem to think that their colleague has entirely lost his mind. If, in the future, literary historians were to tackle the Club of True Creators, we imagine that this very moment will be selected to mark its dissolution.

32

"DAMN YOU, MILOVAN! I will *not* forget this!" Kostreš flings his phone onto the armchair and continues eating fried dumplings.

We gather that Kostreš has been unable to connect with his colleagues, and that this ongoing failure is moreover the cause of considerable distress. At the table with him sits Pešut, whose beard glistens with oil. For the first time since we met his acquaintance, Pešut seems entirely content.

"These might not be exactly like grandma's, but they're not bad, right Rale?"

"Absolutely! Your *pofezne* is fantastic!"

"Do you eat cheese? They're even better with cheese."

"Oh I do, I do, don't you worry," Pešut assures him.

Kostreš washes his last bite down with some yoghurt, wipes his mouth with a napkin, and then gazes intently at his colleague before asking, "Do you remember Teslić, Rale, in the '90s?"

"I...don't recall," Pešut replies, this time with a slight hesitation.

Kostreš pats him on the shoulder, walks to the armchair, retrieves his phone, and murmurs, "Lucky you."

33

ABOUT FIFTEEN KILOMETRES ALONG the route from Raška towards Kraljevo, Milonja has to slow down considerably. Right in front of us, a wrecked Škoda is being dredged from the Ibar riverbed. The scene is so gruesome that most of us avert our eyes from the bloodstained wreckage. Nataša is similarly horrified. She turns her head from the window and whispers, "Poor souls."

34

IT SEEMS THE BAD news has preceded us. Kostreš holds the phone in his hand, as before, now frozen and sheet-white. He sits. He says nothing, while Pešut watches him from the side. The poor man may not know much, but he knows enough to keep any thoughts he does have to himself.

35

A dusk-illuminated road sign heralds Milonja and Nataša's impending return to Novi Sad. The Renault 4's cabin is filled with the oppressive weight of uncertainty. We feel it everywhere: In the unusually sluggish pace of the car, in Milonja's absentminded cheek scratching, in Nataša's pensive gaze out the window, in the rhythmic panting of the dogs, and, most of all, in the total absence of conversation. We all take desperate, deep breaths through the silence, as if trying to slow the seconds on Milonja's wristwatch. Our journey approaches its end at a maddening speed, despite the car moving well under forty kilometres an hour. We fear that all of us—Milonja and Nataša very much included—may be falling inexorably towards our doom. Maybe. Everything has become a 'maybe.' Perhaps, subconsciously, Milonja himself intends to delay his impending meeting with Vuletić. This would explain why he is driving like a blind nonagenarian and coming to a complete stop at every traffic sign.

Ahh, the anxiety is killing us! Chills run down our spines. It's hard to imagine how Milonja and Nataša must feel. If only the silence would break, anything to put us out of our misery...

"I always feel a deep sense of joy returning to Novi Sad," Nataša says, watching Temerinska Street pass by. "But every time I come home, I feel that it's changed, that it's not the same city I was born in... They say that the first sign of ageing is when you say 'it used to be different' or something like that. It's so true. For a long time, I resisted—maybe I didn't want to admit I was getting older. I couldn't process the changes happening right before my eyes. I've fought for as long as I can remember, back to my kindergarten days and this horrible teacher who openly favoured these two sisters.

"She would pamper them like dolls, comb their hair, always putting them at the front of the line on field trips. All the while denying the rest of us any warmth or affection. It was as if, in a society which claimed equality, someone was carrying out a deliberate experiment to introduce children to the real world. Eventually I complained to my mom, and she, along with the other mothers, managed to get the teacher replaced. Since then, I've often told myself, 'Enough, Nataša, it's OK to give up and leave,' but some new injustice is always there to pull me back.

"We have that in common, I think—I've never been able to stomach injustice. Never. I remember confronting a teacher in either second or third grade because she would constantly target this girl Violeta with mean-spirited jokes. It was public humiliation, poorly disguised as humour. I raised my hand and when she called on me, I said, 'Teacher, what you're doing is wrong, and you should be ashamed!' She just about had a stroke. She stammered a bit, and threw me out of the classroom. 'If you're so smart, Žarković, you can go straight to the principal's office!' And the principal of course insisted on the harshest punishment. I'm probably the only student that the principal ever had to reprimand while still in primary school. Later, the teacher got so frustrated that she couldn't make my life miserable—I've always been a good student—that she left our class at the beginning of fourth grade to work at the care centre. And then at law school, of course, it only got worse. A nest of worthless mediocrities joined only by a hollow, shared interest in self-advancement—honestly, it was so depressing, Milonja. I'm sure it's just as bad today, if not worse.

"Motions, appeals, affidavits...I must have written hundreds. Not that they got me anywhere; the university initiated disciplinary proceedings and expelled me. I was this close to filing a private lawsuit, but my father thankfully dissuaded me—pointless, you know? Anyway, I turned tail and left for the University of Belgrade to complete my studies. And of course, with *them* it was my attempt to dethrone their chosen golden boy—somebody's son, with a C-plus average—as student union president. I managed to persuade the wonderful Nada Etinski to apply at the last minute. An exceptional student with a perfect GPA, and an even better human being. But her father was just some farmer in Mošorin, and, on top of that, she was a girl. And this didn't work with their narrative, not at all. They had some thug-in-training confront her in the hallway, threatening consequences for her and her family if she didn't withdraw. Can you believe that, Milonja? Nada withdrew, of course, which

I completely understood. But I obviously had to expose the scandal... Resignations followed, I was expelled... And then it was the '90s; injustice became the very air we breathed.

"I couldn't step outside my door without getting into an argument. I eventually realised that the only way I could keep my sanity was to become a professional fighter for justice, to make it my vocation... And throughout that struggle, I've experienced so much. Moments both beautiful and ugly, crushing disappointments, as well as small victories to keep me going.

"But, Milonja, this situation with Pešut was meant to be my last mission before retirement. I simply couldn't allow yet another villain to escape justice. Someday, I'll show you the testimonials from Teslić... They're monstrous."

Nataša begins to cry. The emotions of the last several minutes overtake her, and she's unable to speak until she feels the warmth of Milonja's hand on her own.

"I'm so sorry... I'm burdening you now... but... before we get home, I wanted to tell you... You know, who you're dealing with..."

"Nataša, we're here."

"What?"

"We've been here. For about five minutes." She looks around through wide eyes, wipes away her tears, and apologises repeatedly. Milonja gathers her in his arms, to reassure her that no apologies are necessary, and says:

"Nataša..."

Had he gone into the movies instead of the police service, Milonja might know the magic words to turn Nataša's spirits around. But not in this reality. He watches awkwardly frozen and says nothing. He looks bone tired.

"Nataša..." he tries again and, this time he seems on the verge of success. "You're amazing. Really."

Amazing? Really? Perhaps he should have kept that one to himself... or... maybe not? A hint of a smile appears first at the corner of Nataša's lips, before spreading across her face. They embrace. Who knows how long it might have lasted under different circumstances, had Milonja not thought to check the time. But, taking Nataša's face tenderly between his hands, he says:

"Vule is already waiting for us at the general prosecutor's office. You need to go in, drop off your things—and the dogs!—take a shower, and be back down in ten minutes. You called your friend to dogsit, she's there already?"

Nataša kisses him, nods affirmatively, and then kisses him again before stepping out of the car. He hands the dogs over to her, along with her luggage, and holds up both hands with fingers splayed. *Ten minutes.*

"Call Father Stefan!" Nataša shouts to him before she opens her friend's gate.

And then, with no warning at all, a SWAT operation explodes into action around us. Four officers storm the house, while three others, shouting, rush to a thoroughly bewildered Milonja and clap cuffs around his wrists. Two police vehicles screech successively to a halt. The cops attending Milonja shove him into the back seat and slam the door, after which it immediately screeches off. Shortly after, two other officers emerge from the house, Nataša between them. She looks back at the house repeatedly until she herself is pushed into the back of the other car, which, within seconds, follows the first in a thick cloud of dust.

Time passes and passes. In fact, an awful lot of it has passed...and who knows how much more will need to pass before we understand exactly what just happened. And how did it happen? And why? And could it have gone differently? Are we, somehow, through action or inaction, culpable? Reflecting on these imponderables, alone in the backseat of a red Renault 4, a conclusive darkness descends at last. We'll have to wait for our answers, it seems, perhaps until morning. For now, it's night, and we've had a very long couple of days.

epilogue

IN THE DAYS, WEEKS, and months that followed, the events which unfolded were largely to be expected...although there were some undeniable surprises as well.

As it turns out, for example, Nataša and Milonja's arrests were not a result of betrayal by Milonja's friend Vuletić. On the contrary, they were the result of a skillfully planned and executed police operation: the deputy general prosecutor felt that the only way to guarantee the pair's safety was to do so from within prison.

With Nataša's testimony, the War Crimes Chamber of the Belgrade District Court filed an updated indictment against Rajko Pešut, and the trial began two months later. The entire process was surprisingly frictionless, likely because Marjan Kostreš found himself riddled with bullets just three days after Nataša's and Milonja's arrest. As the killer made no attempt to escape, the public quickly learned that Kostreš's assassination was connected not to the underworld or covert government activities, but rather a tennis dispute. Kostreš's friend Opalić chose to empty an entire clip from his CZ 75 into him, just as the agent was leaving the SMEČ tennis club. All of this, as Opalić revealed under minimal questioning, was due to wounded pride and a particularly agonising tennis match in which he failed to break forty even once. Kostreš was buried a few days later at the New Cemetery with state honours, "Cesarica" by Oliver Dragojević playing in the background. The funeral was attended by just three rain-soaked colleagues.

As for the aforementioned war crimes trial, Pešut's amnesia had outlasted the doctors' most pessimistic predictions. The testimonies and evidence at his trial were thus a particularly unwelcome surprise. He sobbed unceasingly through virtually the entire trial, emotions running so deep that he begged for summary judgement and a firing squad. The trial continued in accordance with rule of law but, later that night, the mentally shattered Pešut managed to slit his throat and wrists with a razor blade. The details of how he obtained the blade remain a mystery, though it's widely believed a guard might have done him a "favour."

The newest play at the Serbian National Theatre, written by Maja Trnavac and headlined by Slobodan "Boba" Stojšin, was lauded by critics, lavishing praise on script and performances alike. The whole arts community agreed that it was a true dramatic marvel and possibly the National Theater's best performance this millennium. Numerous awards at national and European festivals followed. The comedy-drama "Abduction," in which the playwright describes the trauma of kidnapping from personal experience, earned, among other accolades, the

Sterija Award. Performances in Vienna, Bordeaux, and Athens are already slated for next autumn.

Despite pressure from certain quarters of the arts community, the trial of a group of Novi Sad writers calling themselves the Club of True Creators ended in conviction. The hapless intellectuals were found guilty of unlawful imprisonment by the Novi Sad District Court. Although the prosecution sought the harshest penalties permitted by law, Borojević received just ten months in prison, and even Đorđe and Voja only a year each. Moca, who was asleep for most of the kidnapping, received a three-month suspended sentence. All except for Moca took the verdict very hard, hysterically accusing the judge of conspiracy against Serbian national interests. If the annals of history are to remember Vojislav Počuča's name at all, they will doubtless record his final words as he was dragged from the courtroom: "When the most respected and patriotic Serbian writers are declared guilty, the message is clear—Serbia herself is the one at fault!"

Inspector Šoškić's final case, before finally taking his retirement, was a series of mysterious deaths that were reported throughout Novi Sad by *Večernje Novosti*. In the end, this turned out to be nothing more than a series of fake news stories spread by an underage YouTuber in Salajka. A few months later, Milonja proposed to Nataša and, in a modest but joyful ceremony at the Banjska Monastery, they exchanged their vows. She said "I do" for the first time, and he, for the fifth. Nataša's friend records a video that goes viral within hours. In it, Father

Stefan, as best man, sings "Nebeska Tema" by Idoli while accompanying himself—entirely proficiently—on the guitar.

"*With you, with you, with you, I'm beside you forever...*
We talked for so long, but words didn't matter..."

epilogue to the epilogue

RESTING ON THE UPPER bunk of his prison cell, Vojislav Počuča gazes at his phone and watches the video he made at the very beginning of this tale about the Club of True Creators. A mix of pride and satisfaction shine from his eyes, and his thoughts turn towards a new album which he plans to release entitled "Imprisonment of the Imagination." This, he is confident, will stir up quite a commotion in certain circles when it comes out.

We hear an unlocking, followed by the creaking of a door, while Voja continues his ruminations.

"Počuča, meet your new roommate, Andrić. Play nice, gentlemen," the guard tells him as he leaves the room.

The newcomer looks briefly around the room and then approaches Voja, still lost in reverie. In a distinctly raspy voice, the newcomer says:

"Give you a blowjob, two hundred dinars?"

A chill passes through Voja, who swallows a sudden lump in his throat, and then turns to face his new cellmate.

Everything about that face seems very familiar, from the sunken eyes to the unsettlingly vacant smile. The newcomer gazes curiously at Voja, as if struggling to focus. *Oh my sweet Lord, is this possible?* Voja thinks to himself before crying painfully from his very soul:

"noooO!"

pronouncing serbian

BELOW IS A ROUGH guide to pronouncing the people and place names in Serbian.

The following letters are pronounced similarly to English: A, B, D, E, F, G, I, K, L, M, N, O, P, R, S, T, U, Z.

These letters are pronounced differently from (or don't exist in) English: C, H, J, Lj, Nj, Š, Ž.

And these ones represent sounds that don't exist in English: Ć, Č, Đ, Dž, V

A - f***a***ther

B - ***b***oy

C - ca***ts***

Ć - ***ch***in (Eng), but a bit further back in the mouth, or Mandarin ***q***i

Č - ***ch***in (Eng), but "retroflex" with the tongue curled back, or Mandarin ***ch***a

D - ***d***og

Đ - ***j***oy (Eng), but a bit further back in the mouth, or Mandarin Bei***j***ing

Dž - ***j***oy (Eng), but "retroflex" with the tongue curled back, or Mandarin ***zh***ang

E - p***e***t

F - ***f***un

G - ***g***o

H - lo***ch*** (Scots) or do***ch*** (Ger.)

I - ***ea***t

J - ***y***ou

K - ***k***ite

L - fee***l***

Lj - mi***llion***

M - ***m***an

N - ***n***ow

Nj - ca***ny***on

O - ***ough***t

P - ***p***en

R - quickly rolled, like Spanish pe***r***o or US Eng bu***tt***er

S - ***s***o

Š - ***sh***y

T - ***t***ip

U - l***oo***m

V - Dutch ***w***at, or a cross between ***v***ow and ***w***ow (Eng)

Z - ***z***oo

Ž - lei***s***ure

the balkans of the club of true creators

English Edition

Rossum Press

English Editor

Ryan Davison-Reed

Serbian Edition

Fabrika knjiga

Serbian Editor

Dejan Ilić

ISBN 979-8-9896152-0-9

Milan Tripković was born in 1977 in Belgrade.

He completed his studies
in Serbian and Comparative Literature at the
Faculty of Philosophy in Novi Sad.

He is one of the founders of bookstore Bulevar Books,
and the founding author at Rossum Press.
His first novel, *U dalekom svetu obicnih ljudi*,
was published in 2018.

Printed in Great Britain
by Amazon